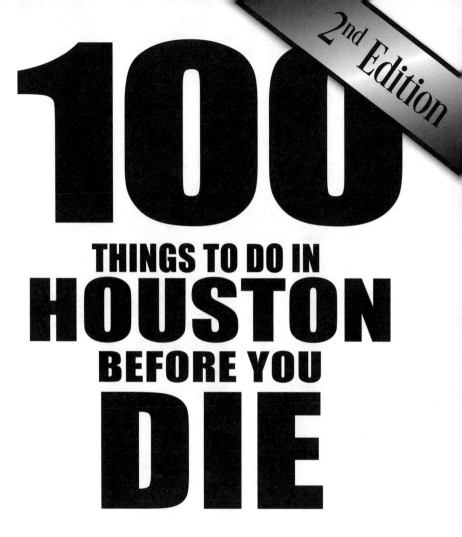

2nd Edition

# 100
## THINGS TO DO IN
# HOUSTON
## BEFORE YOU
# DIE

D0197161

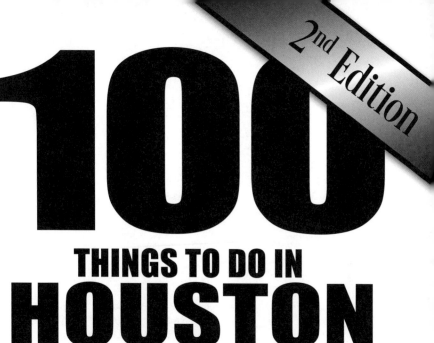

**2nd Edition**

# 100

## THINGS TO DO IN
# HOUSTON
## BEFORE YOU
# DIE

● ● ● ● ● ● ● ● ● ● ● ● ● ● ● ● ● ● ● ● ● ● ● ●

## WILLIAM DYLAN POWELL

REEDY PRESS

Library of Congress Control Number: 2018936117

ISBN: 9781681061467

Design by Jill Halpin

Printed in the United States of America
19 20 21 22   5 4 3 2

Please note that websites, phone numbers, addresses, and company names are subject to change or cancellation. We did our best to relay the most accurate information available, but due to circumstances beyond our control, please do not hold us liable for misinformation. When exploring new destinations, please do your homework before you go.

# DEDICATION

To the survivors: the Harvey house-muckers, the I-10 commuters, the Med Center life savers, the Native Inner Loopers, the new-in-town job seekers, the mosquito swatters, the stay-at-home mothers, the oilfield families, the bootstrap entrepreneurs, the jet-setters, the college students, the corporate warriors, the First Generation Americans, the scheming socialites, the veterans, the tradespeople, the dream-big-even-if-you-failers, the beautiful people, and the hardworking folks who make this city possible from behind the scenes. This is your town.

# CONTENTS

**Preface** . . . . . . . . . . . . . . . . . . . . . . . . . . . . . . . . . . . . . . . . . . . . xiv

**Food and Drink**

1. Raise Your Glass on the Texas Bluebonnet Wine Trail . . . . . . . . . . 2

2. Discover Your Inner Chef with Monica Pope's Cooking Classes . . 4

3. Land That Wristband for the Rodeo BBQ Contest . . . . . . . . . . . . . 5

4. Get Irrational at Pi Pizza . . . . . . . . . . . . . . . . . . . . . . . . . . . . . . . . 6

5. Haunt the Bar at La Carafe . . . . . . . . . . . . . . . . . . . . . . . . . . . . . . 7

6. Spice Up Your Weekend on a Chili Cook-Off Team . . . . . . . . . . . 8

7. Savor Some Comfort Food at Cleburne Cafeteria . . . . . . . . . . . . . 10

8. Fill Up on Fajitas at the Original Ninfa's . . . . . . . . . . . . . . . . . . . . 11

9. Get Your Fresh On at Gilhooley's Oyster Bar . . . . . . . . . . . . . . . . 12

10. Tap into a Legend with a St. Arnold's Tour . . . . . . . . . . . . . . . . . . 14

11. Up Your Brunch Game at Hugo's Sunday Buffet . . . . . . . . . . . . . . 15

12. Savor Authentic Vietnamese All Over Freakin' H-Town . . . . . . . . 16

13. Walk the Wok with Taste of Houston Food Tours . . . . . . . . . . . . . 17

14. Chomp Chicken and Waffles at the Breakfast Klub . . . . . . . . . . . . 18

15. Wait It Out at Killen's Barbecue . . . . . . . . . . . . . . . . . . . . . . . . . . 19

16. Try the Bayou Goo at Houston's House of Pies . . . . . . . . . . . . . . . 20

## Music and Entertainment

**17.** Catch a Midnight Showing at the Historic River Oaks Theatre ... 24

**18.** Stretch Out on the Grass at Miller Outdoor Theatre ............ 25

**19.** Hit Some Highlights on the Cheap with a CityPASS ........... 26

**20.** Learn the Art of Happy Hour at the MFAH on Thursday Nights .. 28

**21.** Catch a Comedy Show at Venues Large and Small............. 29

**22.** Enjoy a Drive-In Movie at Showboat in Hockley .............. 30

**23.** YYYEEE-HHHAAAWWW! at the Redneck Country Club...... 31

**24.** Ride Texas Style at the Lone Star Motorcycle Rally............ 32

**25.** Sample the Renaissance at the Texas Renaissance Festival....... 34

**26.** U-S-A! U-S-A! at Freedom Over Texas..................... 35

**27.** See Amazing Sandcastles at the AIA Sandcastle Competition .... 36

**28.** Knock on the Door at the Last Concert Cafe................. 37

**29.** Witness a Scene at the Alley Theatre....................... 38

**30.** Dance in the Springtime at In Bloom Music Festival ........... 40

**31.** Get Industrious on a Free Ship Channel Cruise................ 41

## Sports and Recreation

**32.** Bun with the Bulls at a Houston Texans Tailgate .............. 44

**33.** Catch a 'Stros Game and Cheer on World Series Winners ....... 46

**34.** Get Some Fresh Air at Armand Bayou Nature Center.......... 48

**35.** Enjoy the Sport of Kings at the Houston Polo Club ............ 49

**36.** Bike, Hike, or Run the "Ho Chi Minh Trails".................. 50

**37.** Get your Groove On with Lessons from METdance . . . . . . . . . . . . 52

**38.** Go Urban Hiking along Buffalo Bayou . . . . . . . . . . . . . . . . . . . . . 53

**39.** Have a Scary Good Ride at the Moonlight Ramble. . . . . . . . . . . . . 54

**40.** Golf the Green Way at Wildcat Golf Club. . . . . . . . . . . . . . . . . . . 56

**41.** Whisper Sweet Somethings into the Discovery Green
Listening Vessels . . . . . . . . . . . . . . . . . . . . . . . . . . . . . . . . . . . . . . 57

**42.** Plink in Style at the Athena Gun Club. . . . . . . . . . . . . . . . . . . . . . 58

**43.** Land the Big One with Galveston Party Boats . . . . . . . . . . . . . . . . 59

**44.** Go Bird Watching at Anahuac National Wildlife Refuge . . . . . . . . 60

**45.** Cheer on the Dynamo during a Texas Derby Game . . . . . . . . . . . . 61

**46.** Go Buck Wild at the Houston Livestock Show and Rodeo . . . . . . . 62

**47.** Shred That Bowl at the Lee and Joe Jamail Skatepark . . . . . . . . . . 63

**48.** Pick Your Own Strawberries at Froberg's Farm . . . . . . . . . . . . . . . 64

**49.** Go Bat Watching at the Waugh Street Bridge . . . . . . . . . . . . . . . . 66

**50.** Rent a BCycle and Roam at Your Own Pace. . . . . . . . . . . . . . . . . . 67

**51.** Push the Button, Burp the Bayou. . . . . . . . . . . . . . . . . . . . . . . . . . 68

**52.** Ice Skate Like a Champ at Discovery Green . . . . . . . . . . . . . . . . . 69

**53.** Make Out at Marfreless . . . . . . . . . . . . . . . . . . . . . . . . . . . . . . . . . 70

**54.** Learn to Use That Camera at the Houston Center
for Photography . . . . . . . . . . . . . . . . . . . . . . . . . . . . . . . . . . . . . . . . 72

**55.** Explore the Heavens at the George Observatory . . . . . . . . . . . . . . . 73

**56.** Ride The Beast at Kemah Boardwalk . . . . . . . . . . . . . . . . . . . . . . . 74

**57.** Take a Selfie in Front of the Water Wall . . . . . . . . . . . . . . . . . . . . . 76

**58.** Get Wonderfully Buzzed at the Wings Over Houston
Air Show ............................................... 77

**59.** Feed the Giraffes at the Houston Zoo ...................... 78

## Culture and History

**60.** Chill Out at the Museum of Funeral History.................. 82

**61.** Sample Old-School Texas Luxury at the Bayou Bend
Collection and Gardens .................................. 83

**62.** Tour H-Town Architecture with Architecture Center Houston .... 84

**63.** See Art in Action at Project Row Houses .................... 86

**64.** Soak Up Some Folk Art at the Orange Show Monument ........ 87

**65.** Cruise in a Masterpiece at the Art Car Parade................. 88

**66.** Experience Heritage at the Buffalo Soldiers National Museum ... 90

**67.** Behold the Power of Print at the Printing Museum............. 91

**68.** Catch a Jazz Age Dinner and Show at Prohibition
Supperclub & Bar ...................................... 92

**69.** Explore the Finest in European Art with a Tour of Rienzi ....... 93

**70.** Find Inspiration at the Washington Avenue Arts District ........ 94

**71.** Catch a Musical at Theatre Under the Stars.................. 95

**72.** Visit Howard Hughes's Grave at Historic Glenwood Cemetery ... 96

**73.** Celebrate Good Works at the Chapel of St. Basil .............. 97

**74.** Reflect on Art as Spirituality at the Rothko Chapel............. 98

**75.** Redefine Domestic Beer at the Beer Can House ...............100

**76.** Visit a Hindu Temple at BAPS Shri Swaminarayan Mandir......101

**77.** Man Battle Stations at the USS *Texas* . . . . . . . . . . . . . . . . . . . . . . 102

**78.** Get a Texas History Overview at the San Jacinto Monument
& Museum . . . . . . . . . . . . . . . . . . . . . . . . . . . . . . . . . . . . . . . . . . . . 104

**79.** Connect with Houston's Past at the Julia Ideson Building . . . . . . . 106

**80.** Mourn the Darkest of Times at the Holocaust Museum Houston . . 108

**81.** Experience Texas History at the George Ranch Historical Park . . . 109

**82.** Get a VIP Look at NASA with a Level 9 Tour of JSC . . . . . . . . . . 110

**83.** Fly Back in Time at the 1940 Air Terminal Museum . . . . . . . . . . . 112

**84.** Peruse Historic Houston at the Houston Heritage Society . . . . . . . 113

**85.** Get Your Zen Back at the Japanese Garden. . . . . . . . . . . . . . . . . . . 114

**86.** Go Underground with a Downtown Tunnel Tour . . . . . . . . . . . . . . 115

**87.** Get the Lowdown on the Buffalo Bayou Cistern. . . . . . . . . . . . . . . 116

**88.** See How Energy Works at Weiss Energy Hall . . . . . . . . . . . . . . . . 117

**Shopping and Fashion**

**89.** Get Ready to Play at Rick's Darts & Games . . . . . . . . . . . . . . . . . . 120

**90.** Treat Yourself at Kuhl-Linscomb . . . . . . . . . . . . . . . . . . . . . . . . . 122

**91.** Wax Nostalgic at Cactus Music. . . . . . . . . . . . . . . . . . . . . . . . . . . 123

**92.** Load Up on Veggies at Canino's Produce and Farmers Market . . . 124

**93.** Buy Some Knockoff Luxury along Harwin Drive. . . . . . . . . . . . . . 126

**94.** Kill an Afternoon at Murder by the Book . . . . . . . . . . . . . . . . . . . 127

**95.** Go Antiquing in The Heights. . . . . . . . . . . . . . . . . . . . . . . . . . . . . 128

**96.** Buy the Finest Boots at Maida's Custom Footwear. . . . . . . . . . . . . 129

**97.** Go Shopping in Asia at the Hong Kong City Mall . . . . . . . . . . . . .130

**98.** Shop with the 1 Percent in the River Oaks District . . . . . . . . . . . .132

**99.** Attend the Quilt Festival Because It's Sew Cool . . . . . . . . . . . . . .133

**100.** Book a Magnificent Suite at the Hotel ZaZa . . . . . . . . . . . . . . . . .134


**Activities by Season** . . . . . . . . . . . . . . . . . . . . . . . . . . . . . . . . . . . . . . . .136

**Index** . . . . . . . . . . . . . . . . . . . . . . . . . . . . . . . . . . . . . . . . . . . . . . . . . . . .139

# PREFACE

Houston is the city you don't see coming. Not until it's too late. Not until you realize how glad you are to call it home—even if just for a day.

It can be said of any city this size (around 6.4 million people in the greater metropolitan area) that whatever you're looking for, you can find it: great restaurants for the foodie, like-minded people for the politically active, niche boutiques for the shopaholic. But this book is about the other things. The things you DIDN'T go looking for, and never knew you needed in your life. The unexpected. The things you can't just find in any old metropolis.

I grew up the son of an oilfield engineer, living in a succession of small towns around various Texas oilfields. But, no matter where we lived, we always ended up coming back to Houston—"energy capital of the world." When I was older and new opportunities in the oil business brought my family to Houston permanently, we had more time to figure out what this city was all about.

The problem, of course, is that this city is so many different cities to so many different types of people. It's simultaneously the kind of place where an artist can live cheaply and plug into a thriving arts community—and also where you can find top-shelf corporate legal counsel, buy a Lamborghini, or hop a charter

••••••••••••••••••••••••••••••

flight to anywhere. It's a religious center. It's a rap scene. It's a hub of technical and engineering expertise. It's home to the world's largest medical center. It's a port city with more than eighty consulates. It's a place where you regularly hear Russian and Arabic and German at the grocery store.

It's the Bayou City. Space City. Clutch/Choke City, depending on how the Rockets are doing. It's "The City with No Limits." It's like having a family of strange and exotic neighbors who keep to themselves; then, when you're finally invited into their home, you realize you've a lot in common and become fast friends.

So step on in—this oddball neighbor has some awesome to share. If you're just visiting, we don't care what you tell your friends back home about Houston. This town isn't about image; it's about imagination. We just want you to be yourself, and enjoy yourself. And if you live in H-Town, why not step out more often? Don't be that person who hasn't experienced all of the flavor that's right around you. Sure, you've done some of these things already, but probably not all of them—and probably not lately.

Now is the time.

••••••••••••••••••••••••••••••

Photo courtesy
of Saint Arnold's
Brewing Company

# FOOD AND DRINK

# RAISE YOUR GLASS
## ON THE TEXAS BLUEBONNET WINE TRAIL

Many people don't realize that Texas has a prestigious wine industry dating back to the 1660s—with more than four hundred wineries! Those familiar with Texas wines think of places like Lubbock or the Hill Country. But just an hour from Houston await seven amazing Texas wineries, all offering something for every taste. An awesome day trip or weekend adventure, this vintage roundup starts, east to west, at the Cork This! Winery in Montgomery, Texas, and ends at the Saddlehorn Winery in Burton (try the cab sauv). Each winemaker along the way offers not only terrific Texas vino but also dinner pairings, concerts, guided tours, grape stomps, and more. The wineries even offer themed trails throughout the year, like the Wine & Chocolate Trail around Valentine's Day and the Spring Bluebonnet Trail, which is a big deal.

texasbluebonnetwinetrail.com

Neighborhood: North-Northwest of Town

## TIP

Get a room, y'all. Remember, what happens in Vegas stays in Vegas. But this is Texas, so designate a driver, keep everyone safe, and don't make it weird.

# DISCOVER YOUR INNER CHEF
## WITH MONICA POPE'S COOKING CLASSES

Want to level up your cooking skills? Learn to take fresh veggies from Houston area farmers markets and turn them into everyday culinary masterpieces. You'll be working with produce harvested from urban farms right here in H-Town, whose products include squash, sweet potatoes, okra, fresh tomatoes, kale, French sorrel, and more. And you'll be learning from the best. James Beard Nominee Chef Monica Pope trained at Prue Leith's School of Food and Wine in London. After stints in Europe and San Francisco, she landed in Houston, where she's helped redefine the dining scene. Owner of casual craft eatery Beaver's, Pope teaches out of her midtown Sparrow Cookshop. And it's BYOB, so if you mess up you can drown your sorrows (better make it a regionally sourced organic wine, though). Great for date night or flying solo.

3701 Travis St.
(713) 524-6922
sparrowhouston.com

Neighborhood: Midtown

# LAND THAT WRISTBAND
## FOR THE RODEO BBQ CONTEST

During the last Thursday in February when the Houston Livestock Show and Rodeo rolls around, 250-plus teams compete in the World's Championship Bar-B-Que Contest. And you've never seen a more exclusive event. The brisket, sausage, ribs, chicken, and such are all a cut above. Then there's the tents. Anyone can go to the public venues, like the outdoor carnival rides or a public food tent called the Chuck Wagon, but the private tents are where the action is. Contest entrants often partner with corporations looking to entertain in a not-so-small tent city erected on rodeo grounds, and you'll need special nightclub-like wristbands to get into each. The tents range from intimate to extravagant, featuring not only contestants' smoky flavorful awesomeness but also open bars, live music, and more. So remember: Come January, Operation Wristband Hunter is a go.

1 NRG Park
rodeohouston.com

Neighborhood: NRG Park

# GET IRRATIONAL
## AT PI PIZZA

Pizza genius Anthony Calleo is a man of many talents, but just one passion: upping expectations for H-Town pizza. Originally run from a truck, Pi Pizza does simple classics to perfection. But its creative combinations will ruin conventional pizza joints for you. The Outdoorsman rocks wild Texas venison sausage and cherries in a port wine syrup. Who's the Mac brings thick-cut smoked bacon and house-made mac and cheese. And the Paneer Death Experience has a turmeric cream sauce, curried spinach, and mustard greens with paneer cheese. With unique adult beverages (try the Screwston Frozen Daiquiri) and super-secret desserts thrown into the mix, the place is legend. In fact, the restaurant has an annual event whereby it offers a free daily slice to anyone who gets a rad Pi Pizza tattoo—and they're never short on takers.

181 Heights Blvd.
(832) 767-2433
pipizzahtx.com

Neighborhood: Heights

# HAUNT THE BAR
## AT LA CARAFE

This tall, narrow building at 813 Congress is Houston's oldest commercial building still in use—dating back to 1847. It's been, among many things, a bakery and a Pony Express station. These days it's an intimate little bar called La Carafe, with a nice selection of wines and a jazz-filled jukebox. La Carafe feels timeless, with lots of friendly conversation, a mellow vibe, and reasonable prices. Behind the bar, an antique cash register sits between two huge columns of melted wax. Fair warning, though: legend says it's haunted. People have reported strange noises coming from the bar's creepy upstairs, mysterious cold spots, flying bottles, the sound of children playing, a "lady in white," and the ghost of a former employee named Carl (whose silhouette is said to be visible on occasion in the upstairs window after closing).

813 Congress Ave.
(713) 229-9399

Neighborhood: Market Square Downtown

# SPICE UP YOUR WEEKEND
## ON A CHILI COOK-OFF TEAM

Opinions differ regarding the chili cook-off's origins, with some people crediting the start of the big Terlingua event in 1967 and others the 1952 State Fair of Texas in Dallas. But everyone agrees they're super fun, and Houston serves up a whole mess of them. Competing is easy. Just recruit your crew, get your recipe strong, prep your stuff, and amaze the judges with fiery awesomeness. Organized chili cook-offs run the gamut between modest affairs and huge, elaborate, hundred-team extravaganzas bringing competitors from out of state. Typically they serve as fundraisers, and Houston has at least one big blowout competition every month. Find them. Serve them. Win them. Hey, it's all the fun and camaraderie of a team sport without having to actually sweat (unless you eat a ghost pepper or something). Pro tip: soak participants in beer for best results.

# THE TOP COOK-OFFS IN TOWN

**Houston Pod Chili Cookoff**

tradersvillage.com/houston/events

**Houston Kosher Chili Cookoff**

houstonkosherchilicookoff.com

**Karbach Cookoff**

karbachcookoff.com

**Little Woodrow's (Midtown) Chili Cook-Off**

littlewoodrows.com

**Houston Roller Derby Siren Chili Cook-Off**

houstonrollerderby.com/index.php/events

# SAVOR SOME COMFORT FOOD
## AT CLEBURNE CAFETERIA

When many Houstonians think "cafeteria," what they're specifically thinking about is Cleburne Cafeteria. For more than seventy-five years, Cleburne Cafeteria has been H-Town's go-to spot for classic American faves like chicken fried steak, turkey and dressing, chicken and dumplings, meatloaf, fried fish, and more. All made from scratch. Your favorite sides are in the house—as well as some originals like zucchini muffins. The city mourned when a 2016 electrical fire burned the place to the ground. But owner George Mickelis wasn't going to let bad luck stand in the way of great food; he worked hard, and in November of 2017 the place reopened bigger and better than ever, like some kind of majestic chicken-fried phoenix. They even threw steaks made to order and adult beverages into the mix upon reopening. Cash only.

3606 Bissonnet
(713) 667-2386
cleburnecafeteria.com

Neighborhood: West University Place

# FILL UP ON FAJITAS
## AT THE ORIGINAL NINFA'S

Ninfa Laurenzo, known around town as "Mama Ninfa," is credited with making fajitas (grilled skirt steak served with tortillas) popular restaurant fare. Laurenzo, a native of the Rio Grande Valley, borrowed money from a friend to open the Original Ninfa's on Navigation, which had just ten tables. She sold 250 orders of fajitas the first day. Eventually the restaurant became a Houston landmark—crawling with the great and the good, including out-of-town celebrities like Rock Hudson, Michael Douglas, John Travolta, and the Bush family. Mama Ninfa passed on in 2005, but her original restaurant is still as hot as its Mugnaini wood-burning oven. Executive Chef Alex Padilla keeps the menu on point, offering not just mouth-watering fajitas but also whole red snapper, enchiladas, ribs, and more. Don't expose the "Navigation Margarita" to open flames—strong stuff!

2704 Navigation Blvd.
(713) 228-1175
ninfas.com

Neighborhood: EaDo

# GET YOUR FRESH ON
## AT GILHOOLEY'S OYSTER BAR

If the world's people agreed on political and economic issues as harmoniously as they agree that Gilhooley's serves Texas's best oysters, world peace would be achieved and every little girl would have a pony. Gilhooley's Restaurant and Oyster Bar is basically a biker bar that serves fresh, amazing seafood. It's a Gulf Coast legend, but low key and unassuming with ramshackle décor. According to *Texas Monthly*, when Guy Fieri demanded a recipe and special tour of the joint, the owners told him to go shuck himself. They don't need PR. They've got what everyone wants: Oysters Gilhooley. To the uninitiated, that means wood-fired oysters with garlic butter and parmesan cheese. Not to mention a stable of Gulf Coast seafood classics done right. And Gilhooley's location makes it a great pit stop while spending a day along the coast.

222 9th St.
(281) 339-3813
facebook.com/gilhooleys

Neighborhood: San Leon

## TIP

You'll have to leave the kiddos on ice for this one—Gilhooley's has a strict no-kids policy. They also don't take credit cards, so just leave your kids at home with the credit cards and an internet connection while you're gone.

# TAP INTO A LEGEND
## WITH A ST. ARNOLD'S TOUR

St. Arnold's Brewing Company was started by a former investment banker and Rice grad who put everything on the line to bring craft beer to Texas. Named after a seventh-century bishop who advised parishioners to drink beer as a way to stay healthy, St. Arnold's is sold only in Texas. Now you can see where the magic is made—including the brewery's primary brewing equipment, which originally came from the Klosterbrauerei Raitenhaslach in Germany. You can choose from a variety of year-round and seasonal brews. (Don't leave without sampling the Fancy Lawnmower.) You get a free pint glass on your birthday, and hardcore fans can join the St. Arnold's Society, for which you get, among other perquisites, free beer for life! Also, try some St. Arnold Root Beer while you're there; making it takes A POUND OF CANE SUGAR per gallon.

2000 Lyons Ave.
(713) 686-9494
saintarnold.com

Neighborhood: Downtown

# UP YOUR BRUNCH GAME
## AT HUGO'S SUNDAY BUFFET

Before you go, ask yourself if you really want a brunch this good because it will RUIN brunch elsewhere. Zagat-rated Hugo's is next level with a Mexican-style feast including chilaquiles (fried tortillas with salsa, eggs, and other deliciousness), huevos rancheros, pork ribs, seafood soups and salads, rack of lamb, and caballeros pobres—a sort of Mexican French toast. Everything is meticulously prepared under the direction of the Ortega family. The dessert selection offers fruits and cheeses, creative cookies, rice pudding, and many types of cake, including an amazing tres leches. And you can enjoy it all while sipping on signature cocktails and listening to a traditional Mexican band. If you try leaving without first having a churro covered in chocolate caliente, your friends will shame you on social media.

1600 Westheimer Rd.
(713) 524-7744
hugosrestaurant.net

Neighborhood: Montrose

# SAVOR AUTHENTIC VIETNAMESE
## ALL OVER FREAKIN' H-TOWN

Houstonians were eating pho before any hipster ever attempted to correct its pronunciation. Our sizable Vietnamese community started with post-war refugees arriving in the mid-1970s who soon became an integral part of H-Town. Good places to start include westside favorites like Nam Giao Restaurant & Bakery, places with snazzy ambience like Le Colonial and Vietopia, and hidden gems like Huynh, Cafe TH, or Pho & Crab. Mai's in midtown is a Houston institution, attendance mandatory, and lovers of the banh mi sandwich should check out Lee's Sandwiches, Roostar, Les Noo'dle, or Les Givrals (where you can legit eat great with just a five-dollar bill). Great pho can be found at any of these places, plus Pho Saigon, Pho Binh, Pho Dien, and more.

Huynh
huynhrestauranthouston.com

Pho & Crab
phoandcrab.com

Cafe TH
cafeth.com

Mai's
maishouston.com

# WALK THE WOK
## WITH TASTE OF HOUSTON FOOD TOURS

Whether you're new in town or just in a rut, it's nice to discover extraordinary places to eat. Taste of Houston Food Tours shows you around some of your future favorites, giving you the inside scoop on restaurants of all kinds—with a little regional H-town history, architecture, and culture thrown in. On each tour, guides who know their stuff will not only let you sample food but also meet the people behind these places while learning loads of interesting facts and local lore along the way. Taste of Houston Food Tours offers separate tours of neighborhoods like Downtown, Montrose, and the Heights. And they change up each experience regularly, keeping things interesting. Best of all? Walking tours help you rack up that step count for guilt-free tasting.

(713) 554-1735
tasteofhoustonfoodtours.com

Downtown, Heights, Montrose, and More

# CHOMP CHICKEN AND WAFFLES
## AT THE BREAKFAST KLUB

Chicken and waffles as we know it dates back to late-night meals at the Wells Supper Club in Harlem. And if you're looking for a perfect execution of this soul food classic, hit the Breakfast Klub. Served with six crispy fried chicken wings, powdered sugar, and fresh strawberries, this combo of savory and sweet is the perfect way to top off a long night out—or start the day with a little decadence. Like all places worth a visit, it's usually crowded with a respectable line. But the line goes quickly (sometimes there's even a saxophonist) and it's well worth the wait. If breakfast just isn't your thing, try the catfish and grits—which many feel is also the best in town for that particular combination. Bonus: damn good coffee.

3711 Travis St.
(713) 528-8561
thebreakfastklub.com

Neighborhood: Midtown

# WAIT IT OUT
## AT KILLEN'S BARBECUE

There has been a line as long as Brewster County at Killen's Barbecue almost every day since the restaurant opened. Owner Ronnie Killen is classically trained, comes from a family of restaurateurs, and has one goal: make the best barbecue. Many discriminating Texans say he's done it, with flavorful brisket, spicy sausage, juicy turkey, tender ribs, succulent pork, and more. The line results from Killen's high standards; he refuses to sell meat cooked past its prime and warehoused until it has a buyer. He carefully prepares and cooks or smokes everything the right way using a blend of pecan, hickory, oak, and mesquite. When something is perfect, it's sold; and when it's all gone, it's gone for the day. The place cranks out 2,500 pounds of meat daily, and usually everything is gone by mid-afternoon. Leave room for dessert and try the bread pudding made with croissants.

3613 E. Broadway
(281) 485-2272
killensbarbecue.com

Neighborhood: Pearland

# TRY THE BAYOU GOO
## AT HOUSTON'S HOUSE OF PIES

A Houston institution since 1967, the House of Pies serves more than forty types of pie made fresh daily. When the holidays roll around, it's like Mad Max Beyond Thunderdome (last year they made ten thousand pies to meet the Thanksgiving rush). Fruit pies, cream pies, cheesecake, all kinds of cake—even sugar-free desserts. And if that weren't enough, the place is also a solid twenty-four-hour diner with full menu. But don't leave without trying the Bayou Goo. This chocolaty, nutty assault threatens to single-handedly put Houston back on top of the "Fattest City in America" list every year. With a pecan-infused crust, it sports a layer of cream cheese, vanilla custard, chocolate chunks, whipped cream, and chocolate shavings on top.

3112 Kirby Dr.
(713) 528-3816
houseofpies.com

Neighborhood: Upper Kirby

## TIP

The OTHER big pie fave in
town is Flying Saucer Pie Shop at
436 W. Crosstimbers Road between
N. Shepherd and Yale. I'm a House of
Pies man myself, but I would be remiss
not to mention Flying Saucer, as
some consider it the sweeter slice.

Melissa Pritchett in the Alley Theatre's *A Christmas Carol: A Ghost Story of Christmas*. Photo by John Everett, courtesy of the Alley Theatre.

# MUSIC AND ENTERTAINMENT

# CATCH A MIDNIGHT SHOWING
## AT THE HISTORIC RIVER OAKS THEATRE

Lots of things have changed in Houston over the years, but one thing hasn't: you can always swing by the River Oaks Theatre for a midnight showing. If you're a movie person, you need this in your life. Built in 1939, it shows only art house, foreign, and indie flicks, and it has a loyal following. It's an awesome Art Deco space right in the thick of the River Oaks Shopping Center, so your dinner-drinks-movie trifecta requires minimal Ubering. But what it's really known for are its Midnight Madness showings of flicks like *A Clockwork Orange*, *The Room*, *Blade Runner*, and, most famously, the *Rocky Horror Picture Show*. It's an old building, so don't go expecting the iPic; you're going to catch an awesome flick in a historic space with a crowd that demands more than the usual Hollywood pabulum.

3601, 2009 W. Gray St.
(713) 524-2175
landmarktheatres.com/houston/river-oaks-theatre

Neighborhood: River Oaks

# STRETCH OUT ON THE GRASS
## AT MILLER OUTDOOR THEATRE

Like the theater but wish you could be outside drinking wine in your comfy clothes? You're in luck. An institution that's almost a hundred years old, the Miller Outdoor Theatre is the biggest outdoor free-of-charge theater of its kind in the nation. What was once a simple columned platform stage is now an elaborate proscenium that's received $10 million-plus in upgrades over recent years, including a $1.5 million sound system. The theater has more than a thousand seats, but most people camp out on the hilly lawn surrounding the stage—sipping wine, snacking, and getting comfy for the show. Productions include symphony concerts, Shakespeare, musicals, traveling dance troupes, kids' shows—you name it. It's also in the heart of the museum district, so you can hit the Houston Museum of Natural Science (HMNS) or zoo, and then an outdoor evening show. Best of all, it costs absolutely nada.

6000 Hermann Park Dr.
(832) 487-7102
milleroutdoortheatre.com

Neighborhood: Museum District

# HIT SOME HIGHLIGHTS
## ON THE CHEAP WITH A CITYPASS

You bought this book, so the secret's out—you're interested in exploring Houston. That means you need a CityPASS, especially if you're new. A CityPASS is a booklet you buy in advance that gets you into five major H-Town attractions at a discount and lets you walk right past the ticket lines. The CityPASS will get an adult or child into Space Center Houston, the Houston Museum of Natural Science, the Downtown Aquarium, either the Houston Zoo or the Museum of Fine Arts, and either the Kemah Boardwalk or the Children's Museum of Houston. Choose any five and save almost 50 percent on the cost of them all! Touch moon rocks, explore life in ancient Egypt, see an original Picasso, ride a rollercoaster, and tire the kiddos out—all at a discount.

citypass.com

## TIP

You've only got nine days to use your CityPASS; plan your weeks carefully so that you don't miss out.

# LEARN THE ART OF HAPPY HOUR
## AT THE MFAH ON THURSDAY NIGHTS

Houstonians spend Thursday evenings in a variety of ways: fighting traffic, binge-watching Netflix, dressing up their cats and forcing them to pantomime Neil Simon's *The Odd Couple*—whatever. But what they SHOULD be doing is hitting the Museum of Fine Arts Houston (MFAH) for happy hour. On Thursdays, the MFAH is free, so you can check out the latest of its sixty-five thousand-plus works and have more money to tip the bartender. When it's nice out, chill on the patio, grab a bite from whatever gourmet food truck is making the rounds, and listen to some music. The museum stays open until 9 p.m. Thursdays to accommodate the crowd (it usually closes at 5 p.m.). It even offers art-themed cocktails, though rumors of the bar serving a Shandy Warhol, Frida Kosmo, and Klimt Julep have not been verified.

1001 Bissonnet St.
(713) 639-7300
mfah.org

Neighborhood: Museum District

# CATCH A COMEDY SHOW
## AT VENUES LARGE AND SMALL

Houston has a thriving, hilarious, you-may-just-pee-yourself comedy scene. But you have to know where to look. Well-known large places like the Improv book big-name acts including Arsenio Hall, Joel McHale, and the odd Wayans brother, while the Joke Joint Comedy Showcase has featured high-profile acts like Billy Gardell, Tim Meadows, and hypnotist Gary Conrad (you are getting sleepy and WILL buy a ticket). But then there are all the open mics on select nights at places like the Secret Group, Boondocks, and Avant Garden. Altogether, these spots produce great comedy practically e'ry damn day. Like to make people laugh? Hey, try an open mic—or take an improv class at places like Station Theater or Houston School of Improv.

Improv Houston
improvhouston.com

Joke Joint Comedy Showcase
jokejointcomedyshowcase.com

The Secret Group
thesecretgrouphtx.com

Station Theater
stationtheater.com

Houston School of Improv
comedysportzhouston.com/school-of-improv

• • • • • • • • • • • • • • • • • • • • • • • • •

# ENJOY A DRIVE-IN MOVIE
## AT SHOWBOAT IN HOCKLEY

The Showboat Drive-In Theater is straight out of the 1950s—only with better audio and less pomade. People line up for the gates to open, then park near one of two separate screens (each showing a different double feature). Kids play in a playground while everyone gets their hot dogs, popcorn, and candy. When dusk hits, people kick back in cars or lawn chairs for a movie under the stars. Tuning your radio to a specific station puts the sound right in your ride, and the lot even has little raised spots so the screen is in full view. Have a truck? Throw an air mattress in the back and get totally comfy. But not too comfy. It's a family place, so save your friskiness for Marfreless. And the best part? A ticket is less than ten bucks!

22422 Farm to Market 2920
(281) 351-5224
theshowboatdrivein.com

Neighborhood: Hockley

# YYYEEE-HHHAAAWWW!
## AT THE REDNECK COUNTRY CLUB

David Allen Coe, Gary P. Nunn, Ray Wylie Hubbard, Charlie Pride, Kenny Rogers, and Gordon Lightfoot have all performed at the popular Redneck Country Club. If you like country music and good Southern cooking and bourbon and basically, America, you'll love this place. Owned by radio celebrity and Native Texan Michael Berry, the Redneck Country Club is an actual country club, with membership dues and everything. Only there's more lawn chairs, Dr Pepper beef tacos, and tattoos than you'll find over in River Oaks. There's even a shiny, real-life General Lee Dodge Challenger on display. Though the parking lot can look a bit like a used truck lot at times, you see all kinds of people at the RCC, and everyone puts differences aside to have fun. It's basically the new Gilley's, only without all the fighting and arson.

11110 W. Airport Blvd.
(281) 809-4867
theredneckcountryclub.com

Neighborhood: Stafford

# RIDE TEXAS STYLE
## AT THE LONE STAR MOTORCYCLE RALLY

In early November each year, four hundred thousand motorcycles roar into Galveston from all parts of the country and transform the island into a scene from *Sons of Anarchy*—in a good way, though, and with real bikers, not just people who look like underwear models. Texas's Sturgis equivalent, the Lone Star Rally, lasts four days, during which the Strand becomes a runway for showing off custom rides. Several dozen concerts are packed into just a few days, with past acts having included biker-friendly bands like Lynyrd Skynyrd, Kid Rock, Uncle Kracker, and, naturally, David Allan Coe. The rally also offers juried bike shows, bike games, classic car shows, competition bike building, a motorcycle giveaway, tons of vendors, and a Miss Lone Star Rally beauty pageant. Organized rides surrounding the event raise money for charity.

Neighborhood: Galveston

● ● ● ● ● ● ● ● ● ● ● ● ● ● ● ● ● ● ● ● ● ● ●

## TIP

No bike? Rent one, or, hey, maybe this is your excuse to buy that Harley you've always wanted. Fffrrreeedddooommm!!!

# SAMPLE THE RENAISSANCE
## AT THE TEXAS RENAISSANCE FESTIVAL

From roughly October to December, five hundred thousand knights, maidens, fairies, wizards, and princesses turn Texas into the sixteenth century. The Texas Renaissance Festival is a massive party with themed weeks including Pirate's Adventure, All Hallows Eve, Barbarian Invasion (Austin politician themed, presumably), and Celtic Christmas. Attendees dress in elaborate period garb, drink mead, shop, watch jousting and swordfights, see tradespeople perform, eat turkey legs, get their role-playing games on, AND CONQUER THIS LAND FOR THE MOTHER OF DRAGONS! Wait, that's *Game of Thrones*. Still, same fan base. Kids love the Ren Fair, and events like the King's Feast make it fun for adults too. For the more adventurous, pitch your tent and spend the night for some neighborly wine, fireside conversation, and the merry sounds of ye olde date night from a hundred tents at once. Huzzah!

21778 FM 1774
(800) 458-3435
texrenfest.com

Neighborhood: Todd Mission

# U-S-A! U-S-A!
## AT FREEDOM OVER TEXAS

Houston's official Fourth of July party draws forty thousand-plus people to Eleanor Tinsley Park and Buffalo Bayou, and it couldn't be any more 'Murica if a giant bald eagle made of other, smaller bald eagles flew in formation overhead. With Tom Cruise riding lead bird. A thirty-year tradition, Freedom Over Texas brings $100,000 worth of dazzling fireworks, multiple concert stages featuring big-name bands, food and cold beer, volleyball tournaments, and awesome aircraft flyovers. People pay for the official party at the park, or just find a patch of grass or rooftop anywhere around downtown. The craziness starts around 4 p.m. and goes until about 10 p.m. The fireworks are coordinated to radio-broadcast music and shown on live TV. Dozens of surrounding cities and neighborhoods also have their own fireworks displays.

500 Allen Pkwy.
houstontx.gov/july4

Neighborhood: Downtown

# SEE AMAZING SANDCASTLES
## AT THE AIA SANDCASTLE COMPETITION

You've never seen a sandcastle until you've attended the American Institute of Architects's Sandcastle Competition. Each year teams of architects gather at Galveston's East Beach to see who can build the coolest, most creative, and best technically executed castle. The event is a fundraiser for AIA Houston and ArCH Foundation; it's actually one of the top five revenue-generating events on the island. For folks like you and me, it's a great chance to gawk at these intricate works, get some sun, and enjoy a cold drink with friends. But it's more than just a day at the beach for the architects and engineers involved, who spend months envisioning, planning, and preparing their elaborate themed sandcastles. The coveted Golden Bucket goes to the best sculpture, and special awards are given out in other categories as well. And spectators always win, having spent a relaxing day at the beach.

East Beach
aiahouston.org/v/site-home/AIA-Sandcastle/3m

Neighborhood: Galveston

# KNOCK ON THE DOOR
## AT THE LAST CONCERT CAFE

There's no sign. Just a bright red door on a nondescript white building off Nance Street. But make no mistake: the Last Concert Cafe is a Houston institution. By day, the Last Concert is a quaint-yet-charmingly-funky little Tex-Mex place with a dark, quiet bar and a large outdoor patio and courtyard. But at night the place lets its freak flag fly as it transforms into a live music venue featuring an eclectic assortment of bands, plenty of dancing, and more than a few hippies. You have to knock twice to get into this Houston original, which first opened in 1949 and was even mentioned by Larry McMurtry in his iconic Houston novel *Terms of Endearment*. The Last Concert hosts shows Wednesday through Saturday until 2 a.m., with people coming from all over town to enjoy the music and friendly neighborhood feel.

1403 Nance St.
(713) 226-8563
lastconcert.com

Neighborhood: Downtown

# WITNESS A SCENE
## AT THE ALLEY THEATRE

The Alley Theatre's history dates back to 1947 in an actual alley off Main Street, leading to the one-room original theater that held fewer than a hundred people. Today, it's one of the top theater companies in the nation, with two main stages seating more than a thousand in its Brutalist-style, Ulrich Franzen-designed building. The Alley brings fresh, innovative plays each year that will make you laugh, cry, think, rally, cherish, and feel grateful to live here. It also offers seasonal mainstay performances like the Summer Chills series, which offers affordably priced murder mystery and suspense productions that get you out of the summer heat, and a holiday production of *A Christmas Carol* that's become a family tradition for many. Subscription packages save you big bucks, and remember: theater isn't just a Saturday night thing.

615 Texas Ave.
(713) 220-5700
alleytheatre.org

Neighborhood: Houston Theater District

**FAST FACT**
The only theater district with more seats in such a concentrated space as Houston's Theater District is in New York City. There are eight performing arts organizations, twelve thousand seats and an untold number of little black dresses squished into this one little spot downtown.

# DANCE IN THE SPRINGTIME
## AT IN BLOOM MUSIC FESTIVAL

Originally known as Free Press Summer Fest, the In Bloom Music Festival features fifty-plus performances across forty-eight hours in March. The original idea was to celebrate local creative talent while having a damn good time. It was the brainchild of *Free Press Houston*, a popular grass roots arts and entertainment publication. In 2016, *Free Press* sold the event to an Austin company that rebranded it as "In Bloom," and moved it to the Spring. You can still find local bands and artists, but now it's a huge destination that brings people to Houston from all over. Jack White, Snoop Dog, Willie Nelson, Wu-Tang Clan, Modest Mouse, Geto Boys, and Dwight Yoakum have all played the festival. And it's a damn good time no matter what you call it. *Free Press Houston* now puts on a different festival, held in December, called Day for Night—which drew twenty-three thousand-plus attendees in 2016.

500 Allen Pkwy.
inbloomfestival.com

Neighborhood: Downtown

# GET INDUSTRIOUS
## ON A FREE SHIP CHANNEL CRUISE

This isn't a romantic kind of cruise (unless you're both chemical engineers), but it's fascinating—and free. Back in the day, Galveston was the big port around here. After a huge hurricane in 1900 leveled the island, Houston seemed safer. So we brought the sea to the city with the Houston Ship Channel. Today its refining, petrochemical, and other facilities bring in around $50 billion annually. The nation relies on it to fuel its lifestyle. Private ships aren't allowed to cruise this strategic waterway, but the hundred-passenger M/V *Sam Houston* has been giving ninety-minute tours since 1958. It lets you see behind-the-scenes glimpses of interesting facilities, cargo ships from around the world, the Turning Basin, and the odd Coast Guard or military vessel. Though the tour is free (as is the coffee), you do have to book weeks in advance.

7300 Clinton Dr.
(281) 883-7710
porthouston.com/sam-houston-boat-tour

Neighborhood: Houston Ship Channel

# SPORTS AND RECREATION

# BUN WITH THE BULLS
## AT A HOUSTON TEXANS TAILGATE

Fans of Houston Texans football are the NFL's most successful, intelligent, attractive, charming, and fun. Just my opinion. But 100 percent fact: game day at NRG Stadium brings hordes of tailgaters doing everything from literally grilling burgers on their tailgates to rolling massive tow-behind smokers. Barbecue, chili, fajitas, pizza, burgers, sausage, venison, boudin, chicken wings, and every other game-day delicacy is represented—some quite fancy. And, of course, plenty of cold beer and margaritas. H-Town was ranked one of the nation's Tastiest Tailgate Cities, and our mild weather means you won't freeze your pigskin off in late fall. Sometimes Texans players and staff even join. In addition to grilling, we get dressed up in full battle gear, dance, play games, kiss our sweethearts, and talk about how the Dallas Cowboys are all a bunch of entitled, good-for-nothin' criminals.

NRG Stadium
NRG Pkwy.
(832) 667-1400
houstontexans.com

Neighborhood: NRG Park

# CATCH A 'STROS GAME
## AND CHEER ON
## WORLD SERIES WINNERS

That's right. World Series champs, baby. H-town fans know how to have a good time, and there's something at Minute Maid for both die-hard ball fans and first-timers. Minute Maid Park was once actually a major railway hub called Union Station, completed in 1911 and designed by the same architects who designed Grand Central Terminal in NYC. The original station concourse is actually now the lobby (you can take a stadium tour). In addition to some damn good baseball, you'll find all kinds of restaurants, street art murals, fancy private party spaces, and places to pick up 'Stros merch. There's even a designated Uber location so you can celebrate the win at the Budweiser Batters Eye Bar right above center field.

501 Crawford St.
(713) 259-8000
mlb.com/astros

Neighborhood: Downtown

## TIP

If you get there early, grab lunch at Jackson Street BBQ next door—or Irma's Original Mexican Restaurant, which has not only great food but also the best lemonade in town.

# GET SOME FRESH AIR
## AT ARMAND BAYOU NATURE CENTER

Know what you could use? An afternoon on two thousand-plus acres of lush nature preserve. Armand Bayou Nature Center is spread out across three distinct ecosystems: forest, coastal prairie, and bayou. Its five miles of hiking trails let you cover all three, encountering all kinds of wildlife along the way (including alligators, so maybe leave the dog at home). It's a great place for bird watching, and the center even offers guided tours for photographers—not to mention a number of themed gardens, a nineteenth-century farmhouse, and pontoon boat cruises. If you're up for a nocturnal adventure, try the night hikes, like the Owl Prowl, Bat Hike, and Firefly Fridays. Best of all, the ABNC is 100 percent, absolutely FREE on the first and third Sundays, so you can reconnect with nature without stressing your budget.

8500 Bay Area Blvd.
(281) 474-2551
abnc.org

Neighborhood: Clear Lake Area

# ENJOY THE SPORT OF KINGS
## AT THE HOUSTON POLO CLUB

Many Americans think of the Northeast, India, or England's home counties when they think of polo. But it's perfect for Texans, bringing together both ponies and drinking. Founded in 1928, the Houston Polo Club is one of the most vibrant polo fields in the nation. It covers twenty-six verdant acres at the southeast corner of I-10 and West Loop 610. Polo is an exciting, fast-paced sport and the matches are a lot of fun—played on a big field but, with just four players to a team, still intimate enough to get into. The public can catch matches Sunday afternoons during the spring or fall. Tickets start at just thirty dollars, with box seating available for business entertainment or special occasions. At the end of the match everyone gathers on the field to stomp divots, sip champagne, and decide which oil and gas stocks to short.

8552 Memorial Dr.
(713) 681-8571
houstonpoloclub.com

Neighborhood: Memorial Park

# BIKE, HIKE, OR RUN
## THE "HO CHI MINH TRAILS"

Everybody knows the three-mile jogging loop around Memorial Park. After all, that's where Houston goes to parade its sculpted bodies and expensive workout gear like tropical birds of paradise out for a jog. But many forget about the other ten miles of mixed-use trails at the south end of the park. Their nickname, the "Ho Chi Minh Trails," is a reference to the jungle paths of Vietnam, and you'll find mountain bikers, hikers, trail runners, and even the occasional horse rider enjoying the lush trails. The environmental transformation is shocking—it's hard to believe you're just a few hundred feet from people sitting in traffic contemplating poor life choices. While you're there, check out the Houston Arboretum & Nature Center to learn all about that adorable animal you saw, whatever pooped on you, and the plant that gave you that rash. Even though most of the trails are shaded, drink plenty of water.

6501 Memorial Dr.
(713) 863-8403

Neighborhood: Memorial Park

## TIP

The Houston Parks and Recreation Department has now color coded the trails, marking them with posts and colored arrows to make getting around easier.

# GET YOUR GROOVE ON
## WITH LESSONS FROM METDANCE

METdance is a not-for-profit dance company composed of elite dancers from across the globe. This renowned organization puts on all kinds of inspiring and innovative performances. Every professional dance company has a repertoire of choreographed pieces, and METdance's portfolio is composed of dozens of stunning works. But it also serves as a dance center, teaching people of all ages ballet, jazz, contemporary, tap, and hip-hop dance—even how to make it as a professional cheerleader. METdance offers classes for kids, teens, or adults. And even though the talent level of the company's artists is immense, it's a very welcoming and supportive atmosphere. Experienced dancers who want to take their game to the next level can even sign up for professional-grade intensive courses or try out to join the company (but you better be pretty darn good).

2808 Caroline St.
(713) 522-6375
metdance.org

Neighborhood: Midtown

# GO URBAN HIKING
## ALONG BUFFALO BAYOU

Buffalo Bayou makes for great urban hiking. You can start way out at Cinco Ranch and hike through George Bush Park, where deer sightings are common. At Highway 6 you'll enter Terry Hershey Park, with trails running all the way to Beltway 8. Along the way, you might see herons and egrets, turtles, rabbits, owls, alligator gar, bats—and maybe even coyotes or bald eagles. Between the Beltway and Loop 610, the bayou runs through private land, soon entering Memorial Park. Closer in you'll find trails along the Bayou from Shepherd all the way to Allen's Landing (including, of course, the 160-acre Buffalo Bayou Park). Altogether it's more than you can do in a day. Kayaking the bayou can also be a unique urban nature experience, but avoid Allen's Landing after dark unless you want a unique urban martial arts experience.

Neighborhood: Katy through Downtown

# HAVE A SCARY GOOD RIDE
## AT THE MOONLIGHT RAMBLE

Looking for something cool to do around Halloween? Skip the bar scene and hit the handlebar scene at the BikeHouston Moonlight Ramble. You don't need a $10,000 carbon fiber bike from Italy, or technical spandex that makes you look like an astronaut. All you need is a small entry fee, a bike with some basic safety gear, and a sense of adventure. Participants not only dress themselves in costumes but also dress up their bikes. Ten- and twenty-mile courses wind through Houston starting at the GRB. This tradition has been going strong for forty-plus years, and the experience comes complete with pre- and post-parties at Discovery Green and cool swag for registrants. The event is a BikeHouston fundraiser, and all proceeds go to the organization's efforts to help keep Houston streets safe for cyclists.

Discovery Green
1500 McKinney St.
bikehouston.org

Neighborhood: Downtown

## TIP

The roads don't close for the ride, and it's as dark as the inside of a pumpkin at that time of night. So make sure your bike is well lit, and brush up on your safety practices and traffic laws.

# GOLF THE GREEN WAY
## AT WILDCAT GOLF CLUB

Just across the loop from NRG Stadium lies one of the most beautiful public golf clubs in Texas. Wildcat Golf Club sports two lush courses: The Lakes offers dramatic elevation changes and lots of water hazards, requiring strategy and finesse. And the Highlands brings tricky bunkers, deep ravines, and an awesome view. Wildcat has a sports bar, valet parking, pro shop, driving range, lessons, and all of the other amenities you expect in a posh golf course. True to Houston, it even has an oil well right out front. But the best part? The whole of the property, both courses, is actually a remediated landfill. That's why it's so hilly. Yup, this fancy-pants place was transformed from a literal dump to a premium golf course courtesy of Republic Services. Greens don't get much greener than that. Fore!

12000 Almeda Rd.
(713) 413-3400
wildcatgolfclub.com

Neighborhood: South Loop

# WHISPER SWEET SOMETHINGS
## INTO THE DISCOVERY GREEN
### LISTENING VESSELS

There's a lot to do in the twelve-acre Discovery Green park space downtown. Ice skating. Picnicking. Sketching people and really accentuating their most prominent facial features to make them more self-conscious. But one of the coolest things is the Listening Vessels. A gift to the city by the late philanthropist Maconda Brown O'Connor (daughter of George R. Brown), this two-piece installation looks like a coconut shell cut into two, each with a seat inside and placed about thirty yards apart. Despite the fact that the vessels are so far apart, people sitting in separate vessels can hear each other perfectly clearly. It's both off-putting and fascinating—a reminder of how sound really works. The technical term for such a setup is a parabolic acoustical reflector, which concentrates sound by way of geometrical acoustics.

Discovery Green
1500 McKinney St.
(713) 400-7336
discoverygreen.com

Neighborhood: Downtown

# PLINK IN STYLE
## AT THE ATHENA GUN CLUB

Whether you shoot regularly or this is your first time, treat yourself to a lane at the posh Athena Gun Club. As a regular shooter at Athena, I can tell you personally this is the nicest range in Houston. It has the upscale leathery feel of a G6 charter jet. Walk in the door and to your left is a world-class gun store with super-helpful staff. To your right is a wall of gun joy ranging from high-end HKs to old school Tommy Guns, any of which you can rent (you can even shoot long guns full auto). They offer gunsmithing services and courses ranging from basic safety and concealed handgun laws to more advanced tactical training—all taught by certified instructors or former military/ law enforcement officers. And the people are as nice as the place, making sure everyone learns and has fun in safety and comfort.

10814 Katy Fwy.
(713) 461-5900
athenagunclub.com

Neighborhood: Memorial/Spring Branch West

# LAND THE BIG ONE
## WITH GALVESTON PARTY BOATS

Owning a boat is a lot of work. And while having a friend with a boat is cool, you're still expected to pitch in with things like gas money or holding a clear-wrapped package under your shirt—just "until we get out of Federal waters." That's what's so great about Galveston Party Boats. This charter service offers half-day Galveston Bay and Jetty trips and longer Gulf of Mexico deepwater fishing expeditions, and you don't have to do anything but fish. All tackle is provided, and deckhands will help with a landed fish or tangled line; there's even a galley with food and snacks. Depending on the trip, you could catch redfish, snapper, king fish, shark, amberjack, and more. The outfit also offers a thirty-hour safari, during which you could land an enormous tuna! Dockhands will even clean/fillet your catch when you get back.

1700 Harborside Dr.
(409) 763-5423
galvestonpartyboatsinc.com

Neighborhood: Galveston's Pier 19

# GO BIRD WATCHING
## AT ANAHUAC NATIONAL
## WILDLIFE REFUGE

Did you know migratory birds use very specific routes known as "flyways"? One of those routes, known as the Central Flyway, passes just east of Houston. The Anahuac National Wildlife Refuge, about an hour from town, is a thirty-four-thousand-acre wildlife preserve built to provide a habitat for birds along the Central Flyway route. Between October and March, thirty-two species of waterfowl can be found at the refuge, as well as osprey, short-eared owls, sedge wren, and other birds coming south. Species like roseate spoonbills, brown pelicans, and whistling ducks also live among the refuge's ponds and prairies year-round. Hike nature trails as you bird watch, picnic, brush up on your photography, fish, and more. During winter migration, up to eighty thousand snow geese can call the refuge home at once! So don't bother washing the car.

4017 FM 563
(409) 267-3337
fws.gov/refuge/Anahuac

Neighborhood: Anahuac, Texas

# CHEER ON THE DYNAMO
## DURING A TEXAS DERBY GAME

Soccer, once viewed by Texans with a disdain traditionally reserved for things like roadside litter and the metric system, has acquired a passionate fan base over the last decade. Texas has two Major League Soccer (MLS) teams, the Houston Dynamo and FC Dallas. Each year they duke it out in a series known as the Texas Derby. And what does the derby winner get? Some lame-o piece of plastic? Oh, hell no. The winner gets El Capitán—an actual functioning replica Howitzer cannon. El Capitán is showcased, and actually fired, during games in celebration of whoever currently has the title. (El Capitán rests comfortably in its natural environment at BBVA Compass stadium as of this writing). Houston leads the series, but it's a close 7–5, so go support Las Naranjas and keep El Capitán in H-Town where it belongs. Let's go, Dynamo!

BBVA Compass Stadium
2200 Texas St.
(713) 547-3000
houstondynamo.com

Neighborhood: EaDo

● ● ● ● ● ● ● ● ● ● ● ● ● ● ● ● ● ● ● ● ● ●

# GO BUCK WILD
## AT THE HOUSTON LIVESTOCK SHOW AND RODEO

In Boston you can watch leaves change. In Houston, you can watch four million accountants, engineers, lawyers, artists, and teachers change into dime-store cowboys and cowgirls. It's Houston Livestock Show and Rodeo time, between the end of February and mid-March. The rodeo offers traditional events like bull riding, calf roping, and all that. There's a magnificent livestock show with beautiful horses, adorable rabbits, goats, cattle, fuzzy little baby chickens, and all sorts of other squee. Then there is the massive lineup of stadium-filling concerts, a wine auction, a barbecue contest, a chili cook-off, tons of shopping, fried Oreos and Twinkies, dances, and rides. You can even take a spin on a mechanical bull! And if you break your leg, just ask the cowgirl next to you for help—she's probably a trauma surgeon.

3 NRG Pkwy.
(832) 667-1000
rodeohouston.com

Neighborhood: NRG Park

# SHRED THAT BOWL
## AT THE LEE AND JOE JAMAIL SKATEPARK

The biggest skate park in Texas, the Lee and Joe Jamail Skatepark totals thirty thousand square feet of ramps, hills, rails, steps, cradles, and other sweet trick-fuel. Tucked into Buffalo Bayou Park just west of the Sabine Street Bridge, this $2.7 million complex has skate areas for everyone, from Tony Hawk (who's totally skated the park) to supervised kids. This place is next-level nice, and not just because of the well-designed obstacles, cool art, or lush park. The people make it nice, too, supportive and welcoming with positive energy for everyone. Totally free and open to the public, the park was named for the late Texas billionaire lawyer Joe Jamail—who had the park built in his wife's honor. It was the largest private donation of funds to build a skate park in the nation's history.

103 Sabine St.
(713) 222-5500
houstontx.gov/parks/parksites/leejoepark.html

Neighborhood: Buffalo Bayou Park

# PICK YOUR OWN STRAWBERRIES
## AT FROBERG'S FARM

Dipped in chocolate and served with champagne, made into a smoothie, or eaten as they come—there's nothing better in the Texas heat than a cool, sweet strawberry. And Froberg's Farm lets you pick them yourself. This twenty-two-acre farm in Alvin grows all kinds of greens. But it's famous for strawberries. Buy a bucket and simply pick the plumpest, juiciest ones you can find. Your bucket is weighed, then you pay. Can't get fresher than that! Froberg's also sells fresh fruits and veggies from across the region, as well as fried pies, jellies, pickles, nuts, jerky, and more. In the fall, Froberg's has a big corn festival with a corn maze, games for the kids, and a hay ride that takes you to pick fresh flowers. Plus, you'll find out what the ever-loving $%&! a "Corn Cannon" is.

3601 Hwy. 6
(281) 585-3531
frobergsfarm.com

Neighborhood: Alvin

## TIP

Watch for rain, since they shut down the self-pick operation in bad weather. Also, leave the dog at home because, as much as we all love dogs, gross. Prime strawberry season around Houston is typically January through May.

# GO BAT WATCHING
## AT THE WAUGH STREET BRIDGE

Many Houstonians love Mexican freetailed bats because each can eat more than one thousand mosquitos an hour. Thanks, bat bros! They're fascinating to watch, and the Waugh Bridge Bat Colony between Memorial Drive and Allen Parkway is a great place to check them out. At its peak, this colony housed more than three hundred thousand bats that would pour out from under the bridge like Toyota Priuses leaving a UT football game. The colony took a big hit during Harvey, but it's still tens of thousands strong and super-cool to watch. The bats keep pretty late hours these days, preferring to come out after dark. There's no set time when you'll see them fly, so you just have to position yourself for go time. You can also hear them chattering about their dinner plans when you're under the bridge (watch your step).

746 Waugh Dr.
Phone Number: Bat Phone

Neighborhood: Allen Parkway

# RENT A BCYCLE
## AND ROAM AT YOUR OWN PACE

BCycle Houston is a citywide bike sharing program with the goal of making H-town more bikeable. And they're doing a darn good job, too. With fifty-one stations offering more than four hundred bikes for short-term rent, just unlock a bike from a BCycle dock, get your ride on, and then return it to any dock around town. Rides are cheap, too—just three dollars for thirty minutes and even cheaper with different membership deals. There are BCycles available all over downtown, the Museum District, Montrose, Rice, Midtown, EaDo, and other locations. There's even an app that helps you find BCycles nearby. It's like having a citywide bike pass. You can rent a bike twenty-four hours a day, seven days per week, and each bike has its own built-in lock. Even Arnold Schwarzenegger was seen recently tooling around on a BCycle while in town.

houston.bcycle.com

# PUSH THE BUTTON,
## BURP THE BAYOU

No sign. No instructions. Just a mysterious red button recessed into an anonymous column on the Preston Street Bridge. When pressed by random passersby, the button causes a ginormous bubble of air to erupt from the bottom of the bayou. What just happened? What did you do? It's OK, no harm done. In fact, the Big Bubble is part art installation, part civil engineering. To keep the meandering Buffalo Bayou from becoming stagnant along this lazy stretch, its waters must be regularly oxygenated. And there's never a shortage of random people willing to push a red button. The bubble actually goes off on its own at regular intervals, just in case there aren't enough people around with the guts to push. Warning: If eructation lasts more than four hours, call your doctor.

Preston Street Bridge
Preston and Smith Sts.

Neighborhood: Theater District

# ICE SKATE LIKE A CHAMP
## AT DISCOVERY GREEN

And when I say "champ," I mean "wobbly awkward baby-ostrich-like thing just out here to have fun because none of us grew up ice skating since this is Houston and it's always eighty-five degrees." Each winter, downtown's Discovery Green opens up more than 7,200 square feet of beautifully maintained skating ice—the largest outdoor rink in Texas. Friends, family, and couples skate along to DJs, live music, and even movies. It's especially pleasant for couples at night, skating beneath the sparkling romantic combination of holiday lights and downtown skyscrapers. And nothing says "I love you" like being willing to fall flat on your face in front of everyone. The rink opens up in December and closes around February. When it warms up? Roll with the season at the Rink: Rolling at Discovery Green, Houston's first outdoor skating rink.

Discovery Green
1500 McKinney St.
(713) 400-7336
discoverygreen.com

Neighborhood: Downtown

# MAKE OUT
## AT MARFRELESS

Marfreless puts the love in loveseat. The most notorious make-out bar in town, it's the perfect spot to take that special someone—known for discretion and privacy (and actual curtains in places). In its current location since 1976, patrons find no sign announcing the place, only an unassuming blue door beneath a staircase behind the River Oaks Theatre. Originally smoky and a bit, well, backseat-like, today's Marfreless is upscale and chic with mood lighting, mellow music, and a well-appointed bar complete with bottle service. Upstairs you'll find more than twenty couches on which smartly dressed couples, and sometimes more than couples, get notoriously cozy. Not lewd, per se. Just, you know, cozy. Bartenders are generous with pours, servers are unobtrusive, the wine list is impressive, and the patrons mind their own business.

2006 Peden St.
(281) 630-6248
marfrelesshouston.com

Neighborhood: River Oaks

## TIP

Leave your flip-flops and ball caps at home. Marfreless likes its clientele sexy these days. And don't forget, you'll be right around some great restaurants and the historic River Oaks Theatre.

# LEARN TO USE THAT CAMERA
## AT THE HOUSTON CENTER FOR PHOTOGRAPHY

The Houston Center for Photography exhibits some of the finest contemporary photography in the world. But it's not just a gallery—it also offers hundreds of classes each year, covering an extraordinary range of topics for all skill levels. These include fundamentals like how to use your camera (finally learn what that button does!) and beginning composition and advanced classes in lighting techniques and portraiture, as well as specialized courses in street photography, food photography, photojournalism, wildflowers, and time lapse. And the facility is incredible, featuring a critique room, a massive photographic library, and a "digital darkroom" where you can learn to Photoshop your online dating profile. Classes are reasonably priced and held multiple days to fit your schedule. The center even hosts master classes, at which you learn directly from guest instructors. Don't forget about the lens cap.

1441 W. Alabama St.
(713) 529-4755
hcponline.org

Neighborhood: Montrose

# EXPLORE THE HEAVENS
## AT THE GEORGE OBSERVATORY

Located at Brazos Bend State Park, the George Observatory offers three huge domed telescopes. The largest is the thirty-six-inch Ritchey–Chrétien-designed Gueymard Research Telescope, one of the nation's largest available for public use. The observatory's East Dome centerpiece is an eighteen-inch fork-mounted equatorial Newtonian reflecting telescope, while the West Dome sports a fourteen-inch Celestron Cassegrain telescope on a Paramount driving platform. All of this high-tech kit brings the wonders of the galaxy right to you, from Saturn's rings to the moon as you've never seen it. And because you're just far enough from the bright Houston lights, you can see the stars clearly. The observatory is owned and operated by the Houston Museum of Natural Science. Its Brazos Bend location means you can really make a day of it, too—hiking and picnicking while the sun is up and stargazing at night.

21901 FM 762 Rd.
(281) 242-3055
hmns.org/george-observatory

Neighborhood: Needville

# RIDE THE BEAST
## AT KEMAH BOARDWALK

With carnival rides, old-school midway games, restaurants, and shopping, Kemah's boardwalk is a fun way to burn a few hours in the summer. But by far the most adrenaline-fueled experience along the boardwalk is The Beast—a beefed-up tour boat that flings groups of tourists around Galveston Bay in style. Powered by two sixteen-cylinder Deutz turbo diesel engines that test out at about 1,300 horsepower each, The Beast punches you out into the bay for the most fun four miles you've ever had on a charter boat with clothes on. The cruise takes twenty-five minutes, and the crew keeps it lively. Yeah, it's touristy. Sure, they pump up the passengers with cheesy rock and disco. But who cares? You will go fast, you will have fun, and you will want to do it again.

555 Bradford Ave.
(281) 334-6640
kemahboardwalk.com

Neighborhood: Kemah

## TIP

Take a Ziploc bag for your phone
because you will also get soaked.
Ladies, consider passing on that
white t-shirt.

# TAKE A SELFIE
## IN FRONT OF THE WATER WALL

The Gerald D. Hines Waterwall Park sits on 2.77 oak tree–filled acres and features a sixty-four-foot horseshoe-shaped wall of cascading water. A cool oasis on a hot summer day, this magnificent installation circulates eleven thousand gallons of water per minute. Water streams down both the inside and outside of its U-shape, forming a small inner courtyard bracketed by an elegant staircase and arched, columned facade. Harvard grad and modernist Philip Johnson and his partner John Burgee designed the installation, with the taps turning on in 1985. Originally called the Transco Fountain because it accompanied Transco Tower (today Williams Tower), the city purchased it in 2008 and renamed the water wall after a local real estate billionaire. What they should have renamed it was Wedding-Photo-Quinceañera-Shopping-Selfie-Romantic-yet-Safe-Place-to-Meet-That-Internet-Date-So-He-Doesn't-Know-Where-You-Live Park.

2800 Post Oak Blvd.
(713) 850-8841
uptown-houston.com/news/page/water-wall-park

Neighborhood: Uptown (Galleria)

# GET WONDERFULLY BUZZED
## AT THE WINGS OVER HOUSTON AIR SHOW

If you see Japanese Zeros, state-of-the-art military helicopters, and acrobatic stunt planes flying overhead, either someone put something in your coffee—or you're at Wings Over Houston. The CAF Wings Over Houston Airshow is Houston's largest, and it brings together premier flying groups from around the country. It's held at Ellington Field just outside the Beltway and has been going on for thirty-plus years. It features rare vintage WWII aircraft, amazing jet acrobatics choreographed to music, NASA planes, Vietnam War–era choppers, and all kinds of rare and exotic flying vehicles. Just pay at the gate, park where you like, and pull up a lawn chair. You can see planes and helicopters close up, just like at a car show, and you can even climb around in some.

wingsoverhouston.com

Neighborhood: Clear Lake

# FEED THE GIRAFFES
## AT THE HOUSTON ZOO

That's right. You can actually feed the adorable, long-eyelashed, neck-tastic giraffes in person. Squee! The fifty-five-acre Houston Zoo is the second-most-visited zoo in the nation (the San Diego Zoo is the first). You can do and see lots of cool stuff there, from exploring the Wortham World of Primates to spying the funkiest frogs you've ever seen. But feeding the giraffes is mandatory adorableness. The zoo built a special Giraffe Feeding Platform with a shaded feeding area, just so you can give the zoo's gentle family of Masai giraffes the snack of a nice, cool lettuce leaf. The weather has to be clear (no rain), and sometimes the giraffes just aren't hungry. But when it all comes together, it's worth it.

6200 Hermann Park Dr.
(713) 533-6500
houstonzoo.org

Neighborhood: Hermann Park

## TIP

Bring seven dollars because you're buying the giraffe chow yourself, but like all charming lunch dates it's totally worth it. Also, check out the Houston Zoo's website for a live giraffe cam!

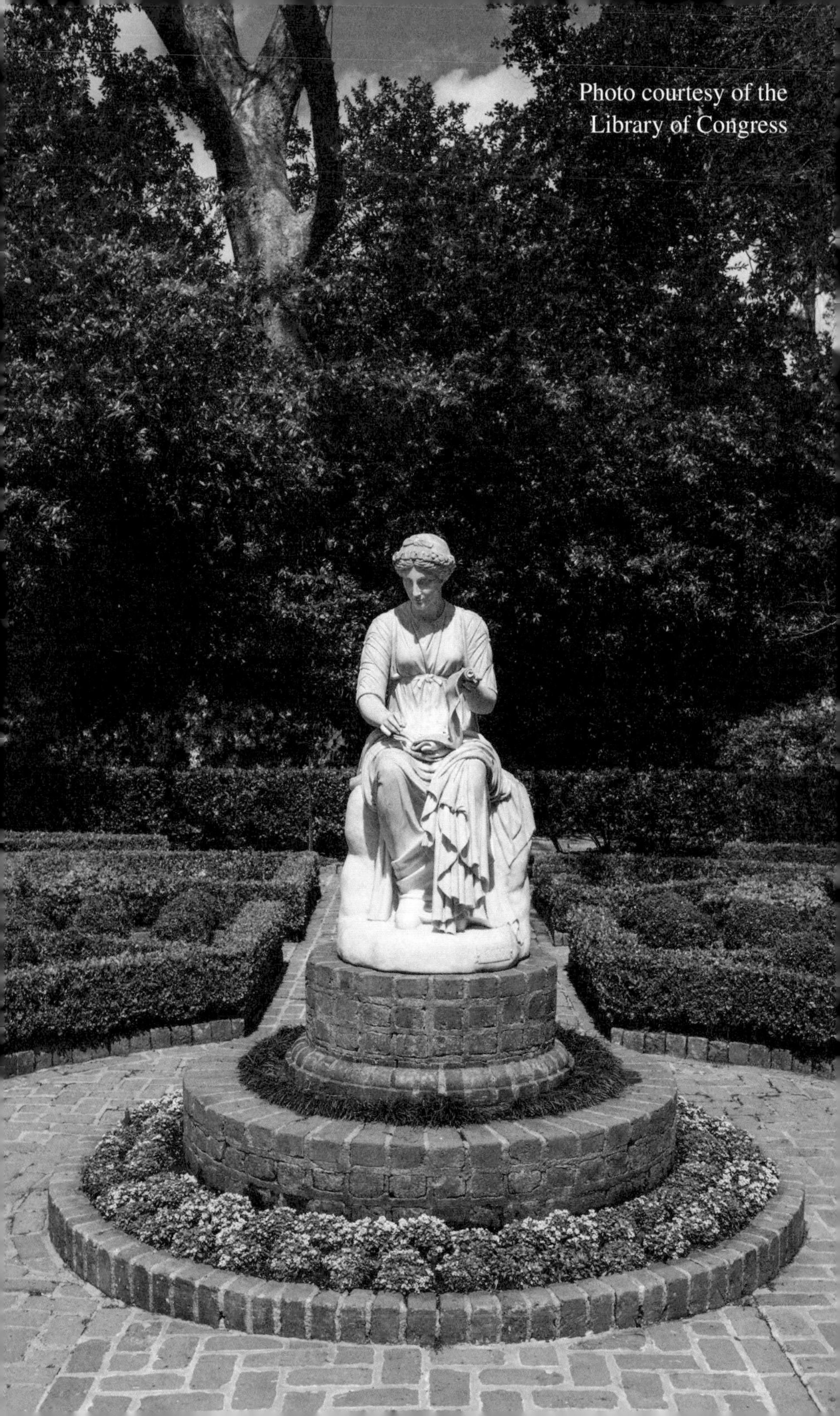
Photo courtesy of the
Library of Congress

# CULTURE AND HISTORY

# CHILL OUT
## AT THE MUSEUM OF FUNERAL HISTORY

Don't make it weird; it's a natural thing. The National Museum of Funeral History lays out all kinds of exhibits and curiosities surrounding one of humanity's oldest cultural rituals. You can explore how people around the world say the Big Goodbye, with exhibits celebrating presidential funerals, Dia de los Muertos, the famous Marsellus Casket Company, and more. You will also learn a bit about the history of embalming, how mourning worked in the eighteenth century, and the funereal traditions of other cultures. My favorite part is all the cool hearses, including elaborate old horse-drawn carriages that will fuel your Victorian Halloween nightmares and a sweet 1951 Superior-Cadillac Landaulet. The museum also has a Batmobile created by George Barris, tying into the funeral business because . . . well, pop culture memories . . . and . . . hey, don't overthink it. Who doesn't want to see the freakin' Batmobile?

415 Barren Springs Dr.
(281) 876-3063
nmfh.org

Neighborhood: Spring

# SAMPLE OLD-SCHOOL TEXAS LUXURY
## AT THE BAYOU BEND COLLECTION AND GARDENS

Bayou Bend is a sumptuously well-preserved and -appointed old mansion in Houston's River Oaks neighborhood. Comprising not just the grand old house but also a vast collection of antique fineries and fourteen acres of surrounding gardens, it's the former home of the late Ima Hogg (1882–1975). Perhaps to make up for that unfortunate name, Ima's father, former governor and lawyer James Stephen Hogg, left her land that ended up generating considerable oil wealth. I'd change my name to Flappy McWaddleFannie for that kind of cabbage. But "Miss Ima," as she was known, put those resources to work making Houston a better place: founding the Houston Symphony, establishing a foundation for mental health, and serving on the school board. She donated Bayou Bend and all of its exquisite paintings, objets d'art, furniture, and more, to the Museum of Fine Arts Houston, which now maintains the place.

6003 Memorial Dr.
(713) 639-7750
mfah.org

Neighborhood: River Oaks

# TOUR H-TOWN ARCHITECTURE
## WITH ARCHITECTURE CENTER HOUSTON

From the commercial Victorian Sweeney, Coombs & Fredericks building to our Art Deco City Hall, Houston has a ton of interesting architecture—and the Architecture Center Houston gives you the lowdown on it all. The group's walking and bicycling tours cover specific neighborhoods, like the Heights and Third Ward, as well as architectural themes that focus on topics including urban art and the origins of different structures' materials. You'll get the history behind the buildings, insights into their designers, and other cool trivia. Tours are just ten bucks, and only half that if you're a dues-paying member of the American Institute of Architects. So get out and up your step count while connecting with all of these buildings you drive by every day.

315 Capitol St., Ste. 120
(713) 520-0155
aiahouston.org

## TIP

The walking tours can last a couple of hours, so wear some comfy walking shoes and drink plenty of water.

# SEE ART IN ACTION
## AT PROJECT ROW HOUSES

Located in Third Ward, one of the city's most historic African American neighborhoods, Project Row Houses is an inspirational intersection of art and community. The site was originally composed of twenty-two row houses, built in the 1930s, that by the 1990s had fallen into disrepair. Dr. John T. Biggers found funding, sponsors, and volunteers to transform the historic houses into art galleries and studios. Hundreds of people pitched in to help clean up the homes and transform them from rundown to uplifting. Today a steady stream of hard-hitting African American artwork is exhibited in the row houses, and an even steadier flow of community support streams from its volunteers and programs. In addition to the visual arts, you can also catch powerful lectures, readings, workshops, and more. Some of the houses are actually set aside for single mothers finishing their education.

2521 Holman St.
(713) 526-7662
projectrowhouses.org

Neighborhood: Third Ward

# SOAK UP SOME FOLK ART
## AT THE ORANGE SHOW MONUMENT

Jeff McKissack loved oranges. Really loved them. So this postman-turned-folk artist built an old-school roadside show in their honor—whimsically constructing the experience himself between 1956 and 1979 using materials scavenged from demolished buildings, roadsides, junkyards, and other places. The walk-through art exhibit extols the health virtues of the orange in a way that would make John McPhee proud. The three-thousand-square-foot environment includes various decks and displays, a stage, a wishing well, and more. Original construction materials included tractor wheels, birds, Texas flags, bricks, plastic dinosaurs, seashells, and mannequins. It's crazy, but a hidden-artistic-genius kind of crazy. McKissack's lifework has blossomed into the Orange Show Center for Visionary Art, a prominent local arts organization that supports a number of arts initiatives and installations. It's a little seedy, but still a-peeling.

2402 Munger St.
(713) 926-6368
orangeshow.org

Neighborhood: Gulfgate/Pine Valley

# CRUISE IN A MASTERPIECE
## AT THE ART CAR PARADE

Port-o-potties, cockroaches, dragons, tiki bars, sharks, and the Family Truckster from National Lampoon's Vacation: they've all been spotted motoring along the route during the Houston Art Car Parade. At one of the most popular events in town, hundreds of teams go outer limits to make the wildest, most elaborate, and super-creative motorized vehicles you could ever imagine. More than a quarter-million people line the Allen Parkway parade route in lawn chairs, watching cars that range from classy-as-hell low riders to giant hippos. Corporations enter cars, but the crowd favorites are always people like me and you who simply get creative. You'll find beer, food, swag, and even an exclusive Art Car Ball held the Friday before the parade. But nobody has more fun than those who create and cruise their own ride or, second best, worm their way into the shotgun seat somewhere.

thehoustonartcarparade.com

Neighborhood: Montrose/Downtown

## TIP

Can't make the Art Car Parade?
Check out the Art Car Museum at 140
S. Heights Boulevard, where you'll find
fascinating permanent and rotating
exhibitions of art cars and other
fine arts projects.

# EXPERIENCE HERITAGE
## AT THE BUFFALO SOLDIERS
## NATIONAL MUSEUM

The Buffalo Soldiers National Museum charts the path of those original post–Civil War U.S. Army regiments composed entirely of African American soldiers. The units got their name from the Cheyenne tribe, who likened them to buffalo because of their curly hair and fighting spirit. The museum tells the story of these fighting men through reenactors, documents, photos, flags, guns, and other cool exhibits. It's a story of American military history, but it's also a snapshot of American civil rights from the nineteenth century. The museum was the brainchild of Captain Paul J. Matthews, Ret. (thank you for your service). A Vietnam veteran, Matthews fueled much of the museum's early exhibits with his own personal collection of artifacts. The Buffalo Soldiers National Museum is housed in the old Houston Light Guard Armory building downtown.

3816 Caroline St.
(713) 942-8920
buffalosoldiermuseumhouston.com

Neighborhood: Midtown

# BEHOLD THE POWER OF PRINT
## AT THE PRINTING MUSEUM

Before you could use your phone to watch a cat get its head stuck in a Chinese takeout box, the power to access and share information or entertainment was determined by who controlled the printed word. Houston's Printing Museum is a monument to that power, celebrating the impact of printing at "the intersections of history, art, and technology." Founded by a foursome of printers in 1979, the museum's collections follow the history of printing chronologically from some of the earliest writings to those retro metal boxy things you see in old movies called "typewriters." Pieces include Mesopotamian cylinder seals dating back to c. 3000–1000 BCE, ancient papyrus fragments (c. 300–350 BCE), illuminated manuscripts from the thirteenth through the sixteenth centuries, and a copy of the *Pennsylvania Gazette* published by Benjamin Franklin in 1765. Make sure to check out their working replica of the Gutenberg press.

1324 W. Clay St.
(713) 522-4652
printingmuseum.org

Neighborhood: Montrose

# CATCH A JAZZ AGE DINNER AND SHOW
## AT PROHIBITION SUPPERCLUB & BAR

The art of burlesque dancing may date back to Victorian London and Paris, but it's alive and well in Houston today, thanks to the Prohibition Supperclub & Bar and its in-house variety troupe, the Moonlight Dolls. Holding court in a retro chic downtown building that once served as Houston's first silent theater, Prohibition gives audiences sexy and exquisitely choreographed neo-burlesque shows along with a decadent prix-fixe dinner. The theater is an intimate space, with dancers interacting with audience goers—even climbing up toward the ceiling during some performances. The Moonlight Dolls bring all kinds of dance, acrobatics, and comedy to the table. While performances are sensual and a bit bawdy, you won't see any actual nudity, and the performers are super-talented dancers, entertainers, and outright amazing athletes. The club's mimosa-soaked "Bitches Who Brunch" Sunday brunch show is also *très* popular.

1008 Prairie St.
(281) 940-4636
prohibitionhouston.com

Neighborhood: Downtown

# EXPLORE THE FINEST IN EUROPEAN ART
## WITH A TOUR OF RIENZI

Rienzi is an exquisite River Oaks mansion filled to capacity with some of the world's finest examples of classical European decorative arts. Owned and operated by the Museum of Fine Arts Houston, the house was built in 1954 by architect John F. Staub for the prominent Masterson family. Sitting on 4.4 acres of immaculate grounds designed by landscape architect Ralph Ellis Gunn, the museum's collections include a myriad of English and European paintings, porcelain, sculptures, furniture, miniatures, and other objets d'art. Its porcelain collection alone would be worth the visit—it's one of the largest collections of Worcester porcelain in the nation. Not only does Rienzi make for a nice afternoon's browsing, but it's also an exquisite venue for an upscale get-together, and you'll find the city's great and good sipping champagne among the rarities. Its chandelier game is strong.

1406 Kirby Dr.
(713) 639-7800
mfah.org/visit/rienzi

Neighborhood: River Oaks

# FIND INSPIRATION
## AT THE WASHINGTON AVENUE ARTS DISTRICT

Painters, sculptors, multimedia artists, jewelers, printmakers, textile artists, metal fabricators—you name it. Only LA boasts more artists in once place than the Washington Avenue Arts District. You'll find open houses, workshops, classes, and cocktails daily, and they're all within walking and biking distance of one another. One of the most interesting studios in the area is the Silos on Sawyer, part of a larger Sawyer Yards complex that includes not just the Silos but also Silver Street, Spring Street, and Winter Street Studios. The building was actually once a packaging facility for Riviana Rice. The facility's thirty-four looming concrete rice silos each serve as an interactive creative space. Altogether, the place spans eighty thousand square feet and houses more than a hundred artists. Each second Saturday of the month, the hundreds of artists at Sawyer Yards throw their collective doors open for a public reception.

1520 Sawyer St.
(713) 868-1839
artsdistricthouston.com

Neighborhood: Sawyer Heights, First Ward, Sixth Ward

# CATCH A MUSICAL
## AT THEATRE UNDER THE STARS

If you're a fan of musicals, check out Theatre Under the Stars (TUTS), under the fresh leadership in 2018 of its new Artistic Director, Dan Knechtges. With shows held at the Hobby Center for the Performing Arts, TUTS is where Houstonians have traditionally gone to catch musical staples such as *Grease*, *Annie*, and *Oklahoma!* But these days it's also pushing its original productions to include innovative new shows, while hosting a number of truly awesome touring acts. The talent and production values set the company apart; you'll find every bit the quality you'd expect in New York, London, or Los Angeles. Founded in 1968, the company takes its name from the original performances it held at Miller Outdoor Theatre (page 25) back in the day. The experience is engaging but not stuffy, and the shows offer something for the whole family.

Hobby Center for the Performing Arts
(ticket office inside the lobby)
800 Bagby St.
(713) 558-2600
tuts.com

Neighborhood: Theater District

# VISIT HOWARD HUGHES'S GRAVE
## AT HISTORIC GLENWOOD CEMETERY

Houstonian Howard Hughes (1905–1976) built and flew airplanes, ran an oil tool company, produced movies, worked covertly with the CIA, founded a medical institute, and owned Vegas casinos. And his final resting place is right off Washington Avenue. The grave is gated and stately, befitting an industrial tycoon; Hughes's net worth was $546 million at the time of his passing ($3.8 billion in today's money). Composed of a small courtyard with a half-circle wall of towering arches and verdant greenery, it's impressive and a great way to celebrate one of the twentieth century's most eccentric figures. To get the most out of your trip, read *Howard Hughes: His Life and Madness* by Donald L. Barlett and James B. Steele before you go. For the scoop on all notable Houstonians in Glenwood—and there are many, including Texas's last president—take Preservation Houston's guided tour.

2525 Washington Ave.
(713) 864-7886
glenwoodcemetery.org

Neighborhood: Washington Avenue

# CELEBRATE GOOD WORKS
## AT THE CHAPEL OF ST. BASIL

You can't miss the gold-domed Chapel of St. Basil off West Alabama at the University of St. Thomas. Near Montrose Boulevard, the structure was designed by renowned architect Philip Johnson. The building's gold dome is actually covered with three thousand square feet of blingy 23.5-karat gold leaf. It's also bisected by a big, black granite wall splitting the worship center from the lobby and letting in tons of natural light. The chapel's entrance is an intriguing asymmetrical slit running up the side of the building that represents the Tent of Meeting from the Old Testament. It truly is an inspiring place, and it serves as an important icon representing the university. Come to see the building, still your mind, or attend Catholic mass, which is held three times a day Monday through Thursday and twice daily on weekends.

1018 W. Alabama St.
(713) 525-3589
stthom.edu

Neighborhood: West University Place

# REFLECT ON ART AS SPIRITUALITY
## AT THE ROTHKO CHAPEL

American artist Mark Rothko was a Nietzsche-fueled weaver of emotions known today mainly for large-format rectangular color fields evocative of the metaphysical. French-born Houstonians John and Dominique de Menil commissioned "the Rothko Chapel," which opened in 1971 as not so much a gallery of his work but a spiritual space. The Philip Johnson-designed octagonal building features fourteen big, powerful, naturally lit Rothko murals in an intimate and impeccably designed environment—serving as an interfaith chapel for personal reflection. You're as likely to find Buddhist monks in attendance as you are black-clad art students. The de Menils were quite the power couple: he an actual French baron and her the heir to the Schlumberger fortune (yes, that Schlumberger, NYSE: SLB).

3900 Yupon St.
(713) 524-9839
rothkochapel.org

Neighborhood: Montrose

## TIP

Ravenous and amply funded collectors of art from around the world, the de Menils assembled a staggering collection that you can explore at the Menil Collection across the park from the chapel.

# REDEFINE
# DOMESTIC BEER
## AT THE BEER CAN HOUSE

The ultimate in H-town kitsch, the beer can house is decorated with fifty thousand-plus cans—many emptied the fun way by their original owner. The late John Milkovisch began creating the beer can house one empty at a time in 1968, initially adorning it with marbles, rocks, metal, and other found materials. He spent almost twenty years adding beer can accents to the place, including aluminum (can) siding, beer can art, wind chimes, a curtain of 1985 bicentennial Falstaff beer cans, beer can garland, and more. He had retired from the Southern Pacific Railroad, so the house gave him something fun to do during his golden years. You can tour the house inside and out, including its collection of vintage cans. Like any good artist, Milkovisch kept his overhead down by drinking "whatever was on sale." Cheers!

222 Malone St.
(713) 926-6368
beercanhouse.org

Neighborhood: Rice Military

# VISIT A HINDU TEMPLE
## AT BAPS SHRI SWAMINARAYAN MANDIR

The BAPS Shri Swaminarayan Mandir looks like it could be in New Delhi. That's because thirty-three thousand pieces of this traditionally designed Hindu temple were hand carved in India and then shipped to Texas for assembly. Built according to strict traditional mandir designs, this impressive Turkish limestone and Italian marble house of worship was the first traditional Hindu mandir in North America. It serves not only as a spiritual center but also an open exhibition in which you can learn more about Hinduism and India's contributions to modern life. The temple features a number of traditional *murtis*, sacred images used in worship. With its towering traditional spires and domes, long reflecting pools, lush landscaping, and peaceful vibe, the BAPS Shri Swaminarayan Mandir is a great place to find a little peace no matter what your religion.

1150 Brand Ln.
(281) 765-2277
baps.org

Neighborhood: Stafford

# MAN BATTLE STATIONS
## AT THE USS *TEXAS*

The USS *Texas* (BB-35), originally launched in 1912, was once the most powerful weapon in the world. It was the first battleship to sport antiaircraft guns, scaring the bejesus out of America's enemies for decades. With a crew of 950-plus, the *Texas* saw service around the world, including Normandy on D-Day. Decommissioned in 1948, she became the nation's first floating museum. Take a self-guided tour and check out the deck, engine room, flag bridge, and more. You'll even find a three-and-a-half-hour Hardhat Tour that walks you through parts of the ship that haven't been restored—the real guts of the thing. By visiting the *Texas*, you can thank her for her service and help fund badly needed repairs to this legendary 106-year-old fighting vessel. The Battleship *Texas* is both a National Historic Landmark and a National Mechanical Engineering Landmark.

3523 Independence Pkwy. S.
(281) 479-2431
tpwd.state.tx.us

Neighborhood: La Porte, Texas

## TIP

The USS *Texas* is moored right by the San Jacinto Monument & Museum (see next page), so you can take in both on the same trip.

# GET A TEXAS HISTORY OVERVIEW
## AT THE SAN JACINTO
## MONUMENT & MUSEUM

Outnumbered and on the run in 1836, Sam Houston's army went from retreat to attack on this coastal plain just east of town. The monument built to celebrate Sam Houston's victory is 567.31 feet tall; 12.31 feet taller than the Washington Monument. Architect Alfred C. Finn, who also designed the Gulf Building, Rice Hotel, and other prominent works, designed the tower, which was completed in 1938. The observation deck offers an awesome view of the former battleground and reflecting pool below. Tour the San Jacinto Museum at the monument's base, which gives a comprehensive, in-depth glimpse into Texas history, including a cool documentary called *Texas Forever!* at the museum's theater. In addition, the monument and its surrounding lands are part of a beautifully maintained state park where you can picnic, bird watch, hike, and more.

1 Monument Cir.
(281) 479-2421
sanjacinto-museum.org

Neighborhood: La Porte, Texas

## TIP

The San Jacinto Monument & Museum offers an app, made in conjunction with the Texas State Historical Association, that you can download to learn more about the battle.

# CONNECT WITH HOUSTON'S PAST
## AT THE JULIA IDESON BUILDING

Built in the 1920s, the Julia Ideson Building was once the city's big central library. Shortly after the new building opened in 1976, the old Ideson became the Houston Metropolitan Research Center—housing thousands of old Houston photographs, manuscripts, maps, architectural drawings, and other cool old stuff. If you're into local history, it's easy to lose a day in the place, and a staff of professional archivists make exploring it all easy. It's also just an incredible space. Designed by architect William Ward Watkin, who also designed the earliest buildings at Rice University and Texas Tech, its Spanish Revival style is homage to Texas's Hispanic heritage. The library's former book storage area is now a gallery featuring rotating exhibits, and the old reading room is an event venue popular for weddings.

550 McKinney St.
(832) 393-1662
houstonlibrary.org

Neighborhood: Downtown

## FAST FACT

The City of Houston has forty-three libraries for Houstonians to use, offering 2.7 million books in twenty languages.

# MOURN THE DARKEST OF TIMES
## AT THE HOLOCAUST MUSEUM HOUSTON

Holocaust Museum Houston is not a fun place to visit. It just isn't. But it's a necessary place to visit, because we owe it to the victims and survivors of Nazi war atrocities. More than six million people lost their lives during the Holocaust, and the Holocaust Museum Houston tells their stories—as well as the stories of survivors who went on to become Houstonians. Its permanent exhibits include a memorial to Jewish communities eradicated by Nazis, a frankly terrifying WWII era railcar, and other thought-provoking exhibits—as well as a number of temporary works. In 2017 the museum began plans for a $33.9 million expansion that will practically double its size. For all its dark content, and actually because of it, Holocaust Museum Houston gives us all inspiration and instruction on how to recognize and fight injustice in our everyday lives.

9220 Kirby Dr., #100
(713) 942-8000
hmh.org

Neighborhood: Museum District

# EXPERIENCE TEXAS HISTORY
## AT THE GEORGE RANCH HISTORICAL PARK

The George Ranch once belonged to an "Old Three Hundred" family under Mexican rule. The family's descendants generously opened their old ranch home and cattle operation so we could experience old-time Texas. You'll encounter different periods in Texas history, including the 1830s (Texas Revolution), the 1860s (War between the States), the 1890s (Victorian Texas), and the 1930s (contemporary America)—all through the eyes of a single family. Period actors inhabit the park, each with their own backstory, going about their daily frontier life. It's like *Westworld*, only offering family friendly historical experiences rather than Ed Harris slapping around sexy robots. Tour historic homes and watch traditional crafts being performed, like blacksmithing and cowboy work. The ranch's history and charm has also made it an in-demand wedding venue for Houstonians looking to share a true Texas experience with guests.

10215 FM 762 Rd.
(281) 343-0218
georgeranch.org

Neighborhood: Richmond

# GET A VIP LOOK AT NASA
## WITH A LEVEL 9 TOUR OF JSC

President Kennedy gave his "we're going to the moon" speech in 1962 right here in Houston at Rice University, and from that moment on Houston's played a major role in space exploration. Today, NASA's Johnson Space Center (JSC) employs around three thousand people, including 110 astronauts. The facility runs, among other things, the International Space Station (ISS), Orion Program, and astronaut corps. The Level 9 Tour is the facility's most in-depth available to the public, given in small groups and taking longer than four hours. Along the way you'll see astronaut training facilities, including the Neutral Buoyancy Lab, the modern-day mission control center where you can watch real-life crews monitor the ISS, and the historic mission control center from which man's first moon landing was controlled. And, because it will be a small group, you get to ask plenty of questions.

2101 E. NASA Pkwy.
(281) 483-0123
nasa.gov

Neighborhood: Clear Lake

## FAST FACT

The phrase "Houston, we have a problem" has shown up in more than twelve thousand news articles and broadcasts since 1982. But it's actually a misquote. The phrase spoken by Apollo 13 astronaut Jack Swigert during the problem mission was really: "OK, Houston, we've had a problem here." The scriptwriter on the film *Apollo 13* with Tom Hanks tweaked the dialogue in the movie, validating the mistaken line.

# FLY BACK IN TIME
## AT THE 1940 AIR TERMINAL MUSEUM

William P. Hobby Airport looks like many airports, with millions of travelers eating Toblerones, staring at their phones, and forgetting where they parked. But look closely and you'll notice the original airport terminal now operating as a museum. A brilliant example of Art Deco architecture, the 1940 Air Terminal Museum offers a glimpse into aviation's past. Its exhibits cover everything from general aviation's earliest days to long-lost airlines. You can even visit a hangar featuring an old Lockheed Lodestar, a 1958 Sikorsky S-58 N887 helicopter, and other cool stuff. It's got a small theater too, and an elegantly fitted dining room popular for fancy parties and meetings. The museum is also a hotspot for plane spotting. Exactly what it sounds like, plane spotting is what aviation enthusiasts call sitting back to watch the planes come and go.

8325 Travelair St.
(713) 454-1940
1940airterminal.org

Neighborhood: Hobby Airport

# PERUSE
# HISTORIC HOUSTON
## AT THE HOUSTON HERITAGE SOCIETY

Traditionally, Houston has been big on profit and shy on preservation. If your family's High Victorian mansion was on prime parking garage land, you pocketed the check and grabbed a sledgehammer. But when the 1847 Kellum-Noble House was up for demolition in the fifties, one group of Houstonians said "Enough is enough" and founded the Houston Heritage Society to save the old home. Today, the Houston Heritage Society plays a critical role in local historic education and preservation, offering permanent and rotating exhibitions showcasing the Houston and Texas of yesteryear. In addition to the 1847 Kellum-Noble House, the society also maintains nine other historic Houston structures downtown, as well as a museum gallery. Enjoy docent-guided tours of the houses, which have been restored to their original condition, filled with historic period artifacts, and transformed into little museums. You can even take a tour on your phone!

1100 Bagby St.
(713) 655-1912
heritagesociety.org

Neighborhood: Downtown

# GET YOUR ZEN BACK
## AT THE JAPANESE GARDEN

Stressed? Stop and stroll through the peaceful paths of the Japanese Garden. Inside Hermann Park just west of the Pioneer Memorial Obelisk, the garden was designed by the late Ken Nakajima, a renowned landscape architect who taught at Tokyo University and designed similar gardens in Montreal, Australia, and Russia. The garden is arranged in the traditional daimyo style, showcasing paths that give you a number of tranquil perspectives and experiences. It's the kind of thing you'd find at the home of Japanese royalty during the Edo period in Japan. This five-acre strolling garden features a traditionally designed teahouse; a cool stone lantern gifted by the city of Chiba, Japan; and elegantly restrained landscaping that makes use of bamboo, azaleas, cherry trees, and more. It's a great place to think, read, meditate, eat, take pictures, or hang with someone special.

6000 Fannin St.
(713) 524-5876
garden.org

Neighborhood: Hermann Park

# GO UNDERGROUND
## WITH A DOWNTOWN TUNNEL TOUR

If you've ever been jostled around Manhattan, you'll notice downtown Houston doesn't have all that many people walking around. That's because so many are enjoying the cool, dry air conditioning of downtown's underground tunnel system. Connecting ninety-five city blocks and spanning six miles, the tunnels let office workers get around without getting out in the heat. Downtown's first tunnel was built in the 1930s as a way to economically air-condition multiple movie theaters at once. These days the tunnels are a complex, color-coded network that includes a number of buildings and routes. On weekdays, throngs of sharply dressed office Morlocks use them to scavenge sandwiches, spread office gossip, and keep up their step count. Prominent tour guide and historian Sandra Lord offers fun and informative tunnel tours essential to H-Town street cred, and you don't want to miss out.

discoverhoustontours.com

Neighborhood: Downtown

# GET THE LOWDOWN
## ON THE BUFFALO BAYOU CISTERN

Consider it urban spelunking. The Buffalo Bayou Cistern is a super-neat underground space that looks like something from a science fiction movie. A water collection and reservoir cistern built in 1926, it was abandoned and all but forgotten for decades as the city's utility infrastructure outgrew it. In 2010, the Buffalo Bayou Partnership rediscovered the place, and in 2016 the underground cement cavern was opened to the public after receiving a $1.2 million grant from the Brown Foundation. Today, the Buffalo Bayou Partnership gives thirty-minute tours of the cistern for just five bucks! It is also a mesmerizing art space, having housed recent exhibits like a cool rain-evoking light show by well-known Venezuelan artist Magdalena Fernández. The cistern also offers a one-hour photography tour, and even meditation sessions in collaboration with the Hines Center for Spirituality and Prayer. Ommmmm.

105 Sabine St.
(713) 752-0314 ext. 301
buffalobayou.org/visit/destination/the-cistern

Neighborhood: Buffalo Bayou Park

# SEE HOW ENERGY WORKS
## AT WEISS ENERGY HALL

Lit up like a forty-thousand-square-foot *Star Trek* set and costing $40 million, the latest iteration of Weiss Energy Hall at the Houston Museum of Natural Science is the most comprehensive energy exhibit on earth. It explains everything about energy, and it does so in a way that's super engaging. Exhibits include "Energy City," a laser model that uses thirty-two projectors to explain how cities get their energy both now and in the future, and the "Genovator," which takes you back in time to see how oil is created. You can also see a model offshore oil rig with cool futuristic-looking equipment, a huge exhibit explaining hydrocarbons, and the "EFX 3000," which transports you to the Eagle Ford shale. Visit even if, and especially if, you don't know anything about oil or energy. It's even fun for non-museum types who just like cool stuff and pushing buttons.

5555 Hermann Park Dr.
(713) 639-4629
hmns.org

Neighborhood: Museum District

# SHOPPING AND FASHION

# GET READY TO PLAY
## AT RICK'S DARTS & GAMES

Most people play games when they're younger—but then stop once they grow up. But with all of our stress and responsibility, adults need playtime now more than ever. That's why Houstonians have Rick's Darts & Games. Rick's is known for its ultimate selection in darts, dartboards, and accessories. But it's way more. Rick's also has a massive and carefully curated selection of chess sets and other board games, kites, puzzles, stuff for disc golf, and other awesomeness. Rick's is also the source for serious "man cave" essentials: poker chips and playing cards, all kinds of cool dominoes, billiards gear, cribbage sets, awesome leathery backgammon boards, and more. They have games you've never heard of. They have games you didn't know you wanted to play. So many games! If you're still not having fun after a trip to Rick's, that's on you.

11396-B Westheimer Rd.
(713) 952-5900
ricksdartsandgames.com

Neighborhood: Westchase District

## TIP

If you're at the Richmond Arms and a British person proposes a friendly wager on a dart game, just don't do it. They're better then you are. Because they're British.

# TREAT YOURSELF
## AT KUHL-LINSCOMB

When it comes to style, it's not what a store sells that makes the difference—it's what it doesn't sell. From tabletop to bed linens, fashion accessories to stationery, everything showcased at iconic Houston style mecca Kuhl-Linscomb has been carefully curated for the most discriminating taste. Owner and interior design goddess Pam Kuhl-Linscomb makes you feel as if you have a personal designer on staff as you walk through her complex of five carefully planned showrooms off West Alabama. You'll find an eclectic assortment of antiques, furniture, fragrances, fine crystal, cool bar accessories, plush rugs, comfy bed linens, interesting books, and lots more. All by some of the finest and freshest brands in the world. And, bonus, for all its chic and sophistication, there's not a snooty attitude to be found.

2424 W. Alabama St.
(713) 526-6000
kuhl-linscomb.com

Neighborhood: River Oaks

# WAX NOSTALGIC
## AT CACTUS MUSIC

Founded in 1975, Cactus Music is an old-school record store. That's right—records. For the fidget-spinning generation, a record is one of those round, grooved discs that spin in front of club DJs while they fiddle with software updates. But it's not so much the inventory that makes Cactus so beloved as the sense of community. Cactus Music attracts passionate music lovers the way Starbucks bathrooms attract . . . eccentrics. Everything about it is awesome—from the selection to the music-themed art and band swag. Almost every Saturday Cactus has in-store live music; Townes Van Zandt, the Police, and the Ramones have all played at the store. People browse the wax, hear about the upcoming shows, and just get their jam on in general. Moves, temporary closings, flooding; nothing can stop the love for this H-Town institution.

2110 Portsmouth St.
(713) 526-9272
cactusmusictx.com

Neighborhood: Montrose

# LOAD UP ON VEGGIES
## AT CANINO'S PRODUCE AND FARMERS MARKET

Dating back to 1958, Canino's Produce and Farmers Market is a fresh food–lover's Mecca. Okra, peppers, onions, watermelon, lettuce, local honey, and fruit preserves—you'll find whatever's in season for sale at the market's numerous vendor stalls that span more than twenty thousand square feet of space. The same local farmers have come from across the region to sell at Canino's for decades, offering great prices (cash only, but feel free to haggle) on food that could have literally been in the ground the day before. You'll also find a number of Mexican specialties that include tomatillos, jicama, nopales, mangos, chilies, and hot sauces. Canino's is right next to El Rey Meat Market, an amazing Mexican butcher shop—and across the street from the El Bolillo bakery and Connie's Seafood Market & Restaurant. Altogether, they make for a fantastic shopping haul.

2520 Airline Dr.
(713) 862-4027
caninoproduce.com

Neighborhood: Heights

## TIP

Local media has reported that this gritty, authentic farmers market has recently been acquired by a private company to transform it into a "destination retail experience." Nobody's quite sure what that means yet, but go see the old Canino's now—then you can say you knew them when.

# BUY SOME KNOCKOFF LUXURY
## ALONG HARWIN DRIVE

Hey, if you're the kind of person to donate last year's dresses and handbags to charity, I get it (see the River Oaks District, p. 132). But for the rest of us there's Harwin Drive. Destinations up and down Harwin include tons of stores whose merchants may have lost the original packaging and haggle like Persian spice dealers. Clothes, leather goods, fragrances, furniture, art—you name it. Are the items authentic? Why would you ask that? A Mont Blanc Meisterstück for ten bucks! Sellers have actually gone to prison in recent years, so sometimes you have to be a regular to access the good stuff. But to be clear, we're not condoning intellectual property crime—merely frugality. Also, tell your husband he's going to want to keep that Bolex Resident watch out of the pool or that's $15 down the bayou.

Neighborhood: Harwin Dr. (between the West Belt and Hillcroft)

# KILL AN AFTERNOON
## AT MURDER BY THE BOOK

Specialty bookstore Murder by the Book is famous worldwide as a hub for whodunits and true crime. Founded in 1980, the shop features twenty-five thousand criminally good titles in stock, including British mysteries, espionage page-turners, cozy capers, noir, thrillers, and much more. But it's not just a place to buy books; it's also a thriving community of readers that hosts book signings, a book discussion group, and even luncheons with mystery authors. It's staffed by passionate readers, meaning solid staff picks spanning a variety of tastes. They can tell you which book to start with in a series, and, after a visit or two, help you find books based on what you've liked in the past. You know—actual expert advice rather than an online algorithm. And you'll find books for every budget, from autographed first edition collectibles to used paperbacks. The game is afoot!

2342 Bissonnet St.
(713) 524-8597
murderbooks.com

Neighborhood: West University Place

# GO ANTIQUING
## IN THE HEIGHTS

The Heights is one of Houston's oldest neighborhoods, and also one of its best places to shop for antiques. Start on 19th Street, where you'll find a number of juicy spots on the same block, including AG Antiques, Gen's Antiques, Retropolis, and Mercader's Antiques. With its small-town feel and walkability, the Heights is a great place to shop, offering everything from rare books to vintage jewelry to ceramic antique dolls that will stare at sleeping guests in your spare room all night long. Aside from 19th Street, don't forget to hit Heights Antiques, August Antiques, Vintage Flea, and Heights Station Antiques. For an added layer of awesome, plan your trip during the Heights's annual White Linen Nights celebration, when everyone decks out in cool white linen and cruises the local art galleries.

AG Antiques
agantiques.com

Mercader's Antiques
mercaderantiques.com

Heights Antiques
heightsantiques.com

Heights Station Antiques
heightsstationantiques.com

Neighborhood: Heights

# BUY THE FINEST BOOTS
## AT MAIDA'S CUSTOM FOOTWEAR

There's nothing whatsoever wrong with everyday boots from the western wear store; I'm wearing a pair right now. But when you want superior quality, you need Maida's. Sal Maida Jr.'s company has been in the business for 115 years, making custom creations by hand with painstaking care and from the finest materials. Maida is a fifth-generation boot maker, and his store is one of the oldest family-owned designer boot companies in the United States. You can see generations of skill in every pair. High-grade leather, ostrich, snakeskin; he works with a number of materials, drawing patterns by hand and putting his heart into the work. John Wayne, Gene Autry, and Mac Davis have all bought from Maida's—not to mention myriad oil and gas tycoons. A pair starts at $750, though considering they may outlive you, it's a bargain.

3733 Westheimer Rd.
(713) 315-7595
maidas.com/boots

Neighborhood: River Oaks

# GO SHOPPING IN ASIA
## AT THE HONG KONG CITY MALL

Houston's modern "Chinatown" is on the west side along Bellaire Boulevard from Gessner Road toward Highway 6. Calling it Chinatown is a bit of a generalization, though, since you'll find the footprints of many Asian cultures. One of its mainstays is the Hong Kong City Mall—a huge enclosed and air conditioned market with Asian stores, restaurants, jewelers, bubble teashops, cafés, bakeries, and more. It's like a quick trip overseas, where you can get everything from a crispy Peking duck for Chinese New Year to Asian books, movies, and housewares. The centerpiece is the Hong Kong Food Market, a big grocery store where you can find not just everyday groceries but a fantastic seafood selection and traditional Asian foods. The complex has some incredible restaurants too, including Ocean Palace (great dim sum), the Crawfish Cafe, and lots of authentic Vietnamese food.

11205 Bellaire Blvd.
(713) 575-7886
hkcitymall.com

Neighborhood: Chinatown

**FAST FACT**

More than ninety languages are
spoken in the Houston area.

# SHOP WITH THE 1 PERCENT
## IN THE RIVER OAKS DISTRICT

The Galleria is great—a world-famous shopping mall. But if you demand more luxury, cross the loop and valet your Bentley at the River Oaks District. This upscale new shopping environment is Houston's fun-sized Rodeo Drive, sporting retail stops like Hermès, Cartier, Chopard, Giuseppe Zanotti, Dior, Tom Ford, and Bonobo. You can grab dinner at Steak 48, Le Colonial (fancy Vietnamese), Taverna, or a number of other fine restaurants. Too fancy? Hopdoddy Burger Bar makes one of the best burgers in Houston. Or, if you've had too much food already, you can catch a workout at the lux Equinox fitness club. Bella Rinova Salon offers luxury salon and spa treatments. And if you want to take in a movie, duck into iPic to see the latest Hollywood blockbuster from the comfort of a luxury recliner.

4444 Westheimer Rd.
(713) 904-1310
riveroaksdistrict.com

Neighborhood: River Oaks

# ATTEND THE QUILT FESTIVAL
## BECAUSE IT'S SEW COOL

If you're into quilting, this is an easy sell. If you're not but still appreciate the arts in general, trust me: give the International Quilting Festival in Houston a shot in the fall. More than fifty thousand people from thirty-plus countries attend this massive show at the George R. Brown Convention Center, where enthusiasts of sewing, quilting, and textile design go crazy (well, as crazy as quilters go, anyway). The work on display is certainly crazy good, though, ranging in style from the abstract to the homey to the political. Hundreds of booths showcase astonishingly detailed and charmingly conceptual pieces for all price ranges, and quilting classes are available. Quilts are entered into cash prize competitions for different categories, and quilters can shop for specialty supplies, fabrics, and other materials. All in all, it's a tight knit community.

George R. Brown Convention Center
1001 Avenida De Las Americas
quilts.com/festival-info.html

Neighborhood: Downtown

# BOOK A MAGNIFICENT SUITE
## AT THE HOTEL ZAZA

At the trendy, upscale Hotel ZaZa, every room is sweet. But not everybody knows that it offers a "Magnificent Seven" of themed suites. The Black Label Suite is more than 2,200 square feet of black-ceilinged elegance with lux furnishings and a two-person bath on the balcony! The ZaZa's Rock Star Suite is adorned with a mirrored master bedroom and pics of famous musicians. And the Tycoon Suite is like staying on a luxury super-yacht that's collected interesting objets d'art at every port. For the more adventurous, try room 322, the "Hard Times Room." This tiny, prison-themed room isn't listed on the website and has been the object of numerous conspiracy theories. It sports exposed brick and, inexplicably, a framed picture of former Stanford Financial Group president Jay T. Comeaux (who, by the way, settled all his SEC claims and wasn't convicted of any wrongdoing).

5701 S. Main St.
(888) 880-3244
hotelzaza.com/houston

Neighborhood: Museum District

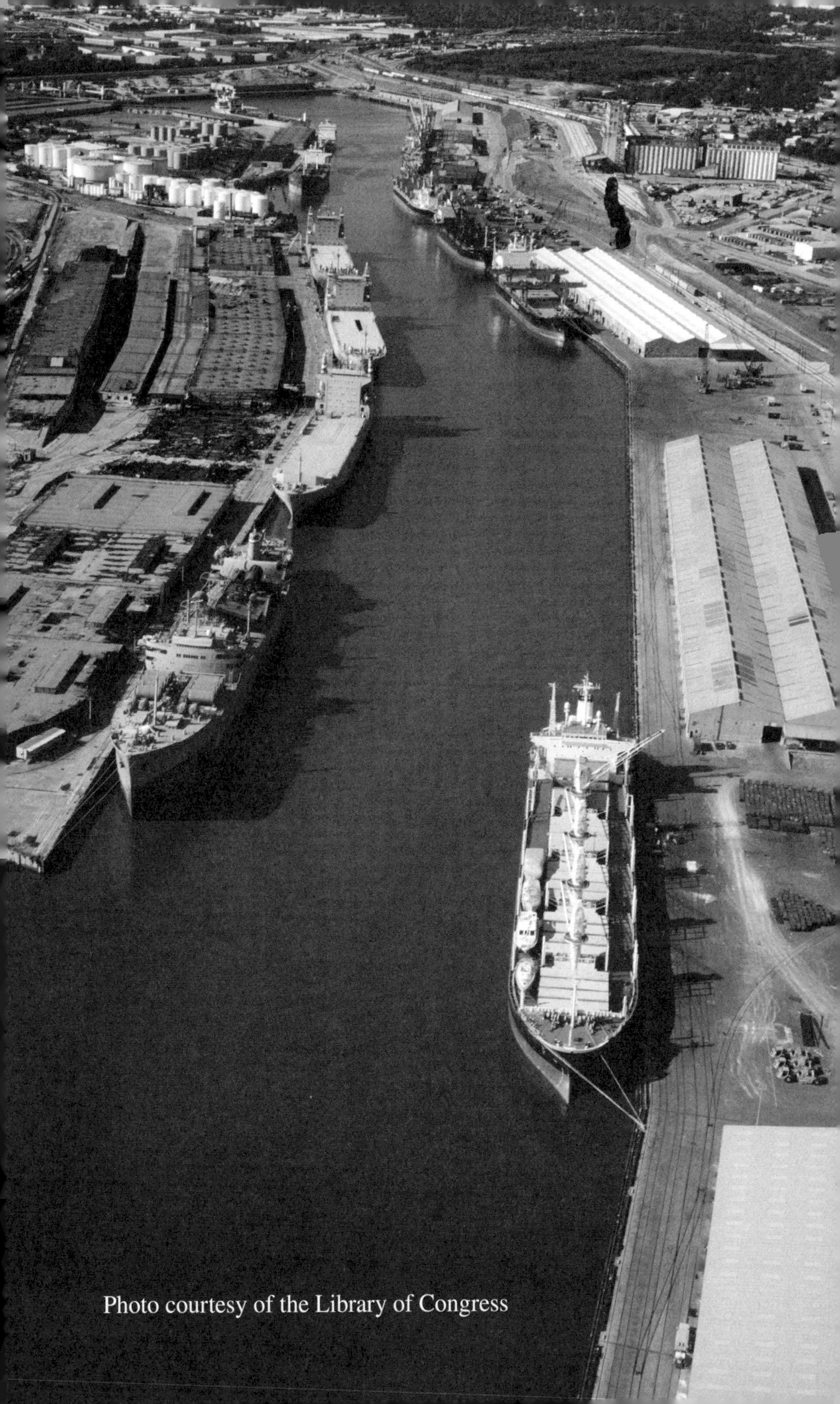
Photo courtesy of the Library of Congress

# ACTIVITIES
## BY SEASON

## WINTER

Get Your Fresh On at Gilhooley's Oyster Bar, 12

Ice Skate Like a Champ at Discovery Green, 69

Witness a Scene at the Alley Theatre, 38

Buy the Finest Boots at Maida's Custom Footwear, 129

Go Buck Wild at the Houston Livestock Show and Rodeo, 62

Land That Wristband for the Rodeo BBQ Contest, 5

## SPRING

Pick Your Own Strawberries at Froberg's Farm, 64

Get Your Zen Back at the Japanese Garden, 114

Make Out at Marfreless, 70

Go Bird Watching at Anahuac National Wildlife Refuge, 60

Feed the Giraffes at the Houston Zoo, 78

Load Up on Veggies at Canino's Produce and Farmers Market, 124

Raise Your Glass on the Texas Bluebonnet Wine Trail, 2

Go Urban Hiking along Buffalo Bayou, 53

Cruise in a Masterpiece at the Art Car Parade, 88

## SUMMER

Golf the Green Way at Wildcat Golf Club, 56

Go Underground with a Downtown Tunnel Tour, 115

U-S-A! U-S-A! at Freedom Over Texas, 35

Stretch Out on the Grass at Miller Outdoor Theatre, 25

Kill an Afternoon at Murder by the Book, 127

See Amazing Sandcastles at the AIA Sandcastle Competition, 36

Ride The Beast at Kemah Boardwalk, 74

Enjoy a Drive-In Movie at the Showboat in Hockley, 30

Go Antiquing in The Heights, 128

## AUTUMN

Have a Scary Good Ride at the Moonlight Ramble, 54

Catch a Midnight Showing at the Historic River Oaks Theatre, 24

Attend the Quilt Festival Because It's Sew Cool, 133

Get Wonderfully Buzzed at the Wings Over Houston Air Show, 77

Bun with the Bulls at a Houston Texans Tailgate, 44

Sample the Renaissance at the Texas Renaissance Festival, 34

Ride Texas Style at the Lone Star Motorcycle Rally, 32

Visiting Howard Hughes's Grave at Historic Glenwood Cemetery, 96

# INDEX

1940 Air Terminal Museum, 112

1847 Kellum-Noble House, 113

Alley Theatre, 22, 38, 136

American Institute of Architects, 36, 84

American Institute of Architects' Sandcastle Competition, 36

Anahuac, 60, 136

Antiquing, 128, 137

August Antiques, 128

Autry, Gene, 129

Avant Garden, 29

Architecture Center Houston, 84

ArCH Foundation, 36

Armand Bayou Nature Center, 48

Art Car Museum, 89

Art Car Parade, 88, 89, 136

Athena Gun Club, 58

BCycle, 67

BAPS Shri Swaminarayan Mandir, 101

Battleship *Texas*, 102

Bayou Bend Collection and Gardens, 83

Bayou Bubble, 68

Bayou Goo, 20

Beaver's, 4

Beer Can House, 100

Bella Rinova Salon, 132

Biggers, John T., Dr., 86

BikeHouston Moonlight Ramble, 54, 137

Bitches Who Brunch, 92

Boondocks, 29

Budweiser Batters Eye Bar, 46

Brazos Bend State Park, 73

Breakfast Klub, The, 18

Buffalo Bayou, 35, 53, 63, 68, 116, 136

Buffalo Soldiers, 90

Cactus Music, 123

CAF Wings Over Houston Air Show, 77, 137

Cafe TH, 16

Calleo, Anthony, 6

Canino's Produce Company, 124, 125, 136

"Carl" the Ghost, 7

Chapel of St. Basil, 97

Children's Museum of Houston, 26

Chili Cook-Off, 8, 9, 62

*Christmas Carol, A*, 22, 38

Comeaux, Jay T., 134

Connie's Seafood Market & Restaurant, 124

Cork This! Winery, 2

Crawfish Cafe, 130

de Menil, Dominique, 98, 99

de Menil, John, 98, 99

Davis, Mac, 129

Downtown Tunnels, 115, 137

Discovery Green, 54, 57, 69, 136

Eleanor Tinsley Park, 35

El Bolillo, 124

El Capitán, 61

El Rey Meat Market, 124

Equinox, 132

Fancy Lawnmower, 14

Finn, Alfred C., 104

Flying Saucer Pie Shop, 21

Freedom Over Texas, 35, 137

*Free Press* Summer Fest, 40

Galveston, 32, 36, 41, 59, 74

Galveston Party Boats, 59

Gen's Antiques, 128

George R. Brown Convention Center, 133

George Ranch Historical Park, 109

George Observatory, 73

Gerald D. Hines Water Wall, 76

Gilhooley's, 12, 13, 136

Glenwood Cemetery, 96, 137

Golden Bucket, 36

Harwin Drive, 126

Hawk, Tony, 63

Heights, Houston, 17, 84, 128, 137

Heights Antiques, 128, 137

Heights Station Antiques, 128, 137

Hermann Park, 114

"Ho Chi Minh Trails," 50

Hobby Center for the Performing Arts, 95

Hogg, Ima, 83

Holocaust Museum Houston, 108

Hong Kong City Mall, 130

Hong Kong Food Market, 130

Hopdoddy Burger Bar, 132

Hotel ZaZa, 134

House of Pies, 20, 21

Houston Astros, 46

Houston City Tours, 17, 41, 84, 85, 96, 113, 115, 137

Houston Center for Photography, 72

Houston CityPASS, 26, 27

Houston Food Tours, 17

Houston Heritage Society, 113

Houston Kosher Chili Cookoff, 9

Houston Light Guard Armory, 90

Houston Livestock Show and Rodeo, 5, 62, 136

Houston Metropolitan Research Center, 106

Houston Museum of Natural Science, 25, 26, 73, 117

Houston Pod Chili Cookoff, 9

Houston Polo Club, 49

Houston Printing Museum, 91

Houston Roller Derby Siren Chili Cook-Off, 9

Houston School of Improv, 29

Houston Ship Channel, 41

Houston Texans, 44, 45, 137

Houston Zoo, 25, 26, 78, 79, 136

Hughes, Howard, 96, 137

Hugo's, 15

Huynh, 16

Improv, The, 29

International Quilting Festival, 133

iPic, 24, 132

In Bloom Music Festival, 40

Jackson Street BBQ, 47

Japanese Garden, 114, 136

Johnson, Philip, 76, 97, 98

Joke Joint Comedy Showcase, 29

Johnson Space Center, 26, 110

Julia Ideson Building, 106

Kemah Boardwalk, 26, 74, 137

Kennedy, John F., 110

Killen's Barbecue, 19

Killen, Ronnie, 19

Knechtges, Dan, 95

Kuhl-Linscomb, 122

Kuhl-Linscomb, Pam, 122

La Carafe, 7

Le Colonial, 16, 132

Le Viet, 16

Last Concert Cafe, 37

Laurenzo, Ninfa, 11

Lee and Joe Jamail Skatepark, 63

Lee's Sandwiches, 16

Les Givrals, 16

Les Noo'dle, 16

Level 9 Tour, 110

Little Woodrow's (Midtown) Chili Cook-Off, 9

Listening Vessels, 57

Lone Star Motorcycle Rally, 32, 137

Lord, Sandra, 115

Mai's, 16

Maida's, 129, 136

Marfreless, 30, 70, 71, 136

Margaritas, 44

Matthews, Paul J. (Capt., Ret.), 90

McKissack, Jeff, 87

McMurtry, Larry, 37

Memorial Park, 50, 53

Menil Collection, The, 99

Mercader's Antiques, 128

METdance, 52

Mickelis, George, 10

Milkovisch, John, 100

Miller Outdoor Theatre, 25, 95, 137

Minute Maid Park, 46

Murder by the Book, 127, 137

Museum of Fine Arts, Houston, 26, 28, 83, 93

NASA, 77, 110

Nakajima, Ken, 114

Nam Giao Restaurant & Bakery, 16

Navigation Margarita, 11

Ninfa's, 11

NRG Stadium, 44, 56

Ocean Palace, 130

Orange Show Center for Visionary Art, 87

Ortega, Hugo, 15

Ortega, Ruben, 15

Preston Street Bridge, 68

Pho & Crab, 16

Pho Binh, 16

Pho Dien, 16

Pho Saigon, 16

Pi Pizza, 6

Pope, Monica, 4

Preservation Houston, 96

Prohibition Supperclub & Bar, 92

Project Row Houses, 86

Redneck Country Club, 31

Retropolis, 128

Republic Services, 56

Rice University, 106, 110

Rick's Darts & Games, 120

Rienzi, 93

River Oaks, 31, 83, 93, 126, 132

River Oaks Theatre, 24, 70, 71, 137

River Oaks Shopping Center, 24

*Rocky Horror Picture Show*, 24

Rothko Chapel, 98

Rothko, Mark, 98

Roostar, 16

Saddlehorn Winery, 2

San Jacinto Monument & Museum, 103, 104, 105

Sawyer Yards, 94

Schlumberger, 98

Secret Group, The, 29

Showboat Drive-In Theater, 30, 137

Silos on Sawyer, The, 94

Silver Street, 94

Space Center Houston, 26

Sparrow Bar + Cookshop, 4

Spring Bluebonnet Trail, 2

Spring Street, 94

St. Arnold's Brewing Company, 14

Staub, John F., 93

Station Theater, 29

Steak 48, 132

Summer Chills Series, 38

Taste of Houston Food Tours, 17

Taverna, 132

Texas Bluebonnet Wine Trail, 2, 136

Texas Derby, 61

Texas Renaissance Festival, 34, 137

Theatre Under the Stars, 95

Vietopia, 16

Vintage Flea, 128

Water Wall, The, 76

Washington Avenue Arts District, 94

Waugh Bridge Bat Colony, 66

Wayne, John, 129

Wells Supper Club, 18

Weiss Energy Hall, 117

White Linen Nights, 128

Wildcat Golf Club, 56, 137

Wine & Chocolate Trail, 2

Winter Street, 94

Worcester porcelain, 93

World's Championship Bar-B-Que Contest, 5